DON'T GROW OI

BY

DOROTHY CARNEGIE

HOW TO HELP YOUR HUSBAND GET AHEAD IN HIS
SOCIAL AND BUSINESS LIFE

DON'T GROW OLD—GROW UP!

Don't Grow Old— Grow Up!

by DOROTHY CARNEGIE

PRESIDENT,

DALE CARNEGIE AND ASSOCIATES, INC.

E. P. DUTTON

NEW YORK

*Published in the United States by E.P. Dutton, a
division of NAL Penguin Inc., 2 Park Avenue,
New York, N.Y. 10016.*

A portion of this book originally appeared in
American Weekly.

Library of Congress Catalog Card No.: 56-6307
ISBN: 0-525-09455-5

30   29   28   27   25

I want to express my gratitude and appreciation to Robert H. Prall for his valuable contribution in preparing this book.

DOROTHY CARNEGIE

CONTENTS

INTRODUCTION

I have on my desk a newspaper clipping which reads: "University of Chicago scientists are trying to measure a man's age by 'maturity' instead of years. They will find that all grow old but few grow up."

Until fairly recently, the word "maturity" has not been in the language of compliment. To call a woman "mature" has been uncomfortably akin in her mind, at least, to labeling her fat, dowdy and void of sex appeal.

Economically and socially, our national accent is on youth. The secret dream of every woman is to look twenty-five forever. The saleswoman's most potent adjective is "youthful." Our advertising is based to a great extent on the common desire to look, act and feel young. Men may not display this desire as openly as do women, but they are equally concerned with retaining their youth. Every golf course is loaded with its week-end quota of forty-plus laddies in perspiring pursuit of the lost waistline of their twenties—and they are as diet-conscious as their wives.

Nor is staying young merely an obsession of the frivolous. At present, it is an economic necessity. Compulsory retirement age in business and industry is still sixty-five, in most cases, and for the average wage earner jobs are increasingly hard to land after the age of thirty-five.

America is a land of youth-worshipers. In older civilizations, women past middle age are still acknowledged beautiful, charming and desirable, and men of sixty-plus are conceded wise and worshipful. Perhaps our attitude is merely a reflection of our nation's comparative youth. But, whatever the cause, the results are plainly evident: we are cheating ourselves, individually and collectively, out of the rewards of maturity by a puerile refusal to grow up and behave like adults.

Youth, for all its attractiveness, is only preparation for adulthood, a rehearsal period for the drama of life. To deny one's manhood or womanhood by desiring to live in a state of perpetual youth is an infantile attempt to stave off responsibility for facing life as a full-grown human being.

The desire for fulfillment, for using ourselves and our abilities, is the desire for maturity. Maturity is growing up. And that dreaded old age sets in when we cease to grow. The very phrase, "growing old," is a contradiction. Old age sets in only when there is no longer any growth of mind or personality. As long as we are learning, developing, contributing, producing or enjoying, we are maturing, whether we are sixteen or ninety-six. We become old when we are no longer capable of improvement, regardless of calendar years.

This book is offered as a guidebook to some of the important areas of life, such as social and marital relations, in which a mature approach is most necessary and desirable. It also discusses certain attitudes toward life which seem to me to be fundamental to the mature mind.

My purpose is to emphasize the rewards of maturity and to point out ways of achieving it; to encourage people to regard life as a growing-up process, not a steady downward progression of decline and decay. I believe that maturity is what we should all strive to achieve and that this desire for growth and wisdom should dominate any other goals we may set up for ourselves.

Whenever possible, I have tried to illustrate my points with real stories about real people. Most of these people have been students of the Dale Carnegie Course in Effective Speaking and Human Relations. I am most grateful to them for having given me permission to use their testimonies in this book.

I hope that the ideas expressed in the following pages will offer a substitute for the popular let's-stay-young philosophy. I would like to see the time come when qualities of mind and spirit are considered as glamorous and desirable as an unlined face or resilient muscle tone; when to be considered mature and wise brings more pleasure than to be told we look ten years younger; and when nobody is ever considered by himself or others to be too old for anything he feels capable or desirous of doing. If this happy state of things ever comes about, we will no longer fear growing old. We will be grown up!

Dorothy Carnegie

PART **one**

THE FIRST STEP TOWARD MATURITY–RESPONSIBILITY

1

DON'T KICK THE CHAIR

ONE DAY MY TODDLER, Donna Dale, carried her little chair to the kitchen and tried to climb to the top of the refrigerator. I rushed to the rescue, but not in time to save her from a crash landing. As I picked her up, she managed to deliver a healthy kick to the chair, while she bellowed:

"Bad old chair made me fall!"

If you have been exposed to small children, you have heard the same excuse many times. A baby just does what comes naturally. Blaming inaminate objects or innocent bystanders for his tumbles is normal behavior for him.

Trouble comes, however, when we carry this childish reaction into adulthood. The tendency to blame others for our own failures and mistakes is as old as mankind. Even Adam excused himself by putting the blame on Eve: "The woman tempted me and I did eat."

The first step toward maturity is to accept responsibility for ourselves, to face life with the conviction that we are no longer children looking for a chair to kick when we trip and fall.

It is much easier, of course, not to do this. It is easier to blame our parents, our boss, our teachers, our environment, our husband, our wife, our children. We can even blame our ancestors, the government in Washington or, if we still need an alibi, Lady Luck herself.

To the immature, there is always some reason—outside of themselves, naturally—for their own shortcomings and disasters. They had a wretched childhood. Their parents were too poor or too rich, too strict or too lax. They never had an education. They've always suffered from poor health.

Their wives, or their husbands, don't understand them. They never got the breaks and the odds were always against them. It is surprising how the whole universe conspires to make things tough for these people. The idea of overcoming difficulties instead of finding a convenient scapegoat never seems to enter their heads.

I remember a student in one of our classes who came to me one day after the other students had left. We had been training the class to learn to remember people's names on that particular day. This woman said to me:

"Mrs. Carnegie, I hope you don't expect me to improve my memory for names. That's one thing I positively cannot do."

"Why not?" I asked her.

"It runs in the family," she answered. "All of us have a poor memory. I inherited it from my mother and father. So you see, I cannot possibly make much of a showing in this respect."

"Miss ———," I said, "your trouble isn't inheritance; it's laziness. You find it easier to blame your family than to make the mental effort necessary to improve your memory. Sit down and I'll prove it to you."

I drilled this woman on a few simple memory exercises for the next several minutes and, because she was concentrating, she did very well. It took some time to rid her of the notion that she couldn't train her mind better than her ancestors had done. But she did, I am glad to report, finally learn to improve her memory instead of excusing it.

Parents these days are lucky not to be blamed for more than poor memories. It seems fashionable to blame them for everything from falling hair to frustrations.

For example, I know one young woman who is quite outspoken about how her mother has affected her life. The mother was left a widow when the girl was a baby. She had to go to work to support herself and her child. Through ability and hard work, she became a successful businesswoman. Her daughter was reared with love, care and every educational advantage. But that, apparently, was not enough. The great cross this daughter has to bear is—guess what? Mother's success!

The poor girl claims that her youth has been blighted because she feels what she calls a "sense of competition" with her mother. And the bewildered mother says:

"I don't understand Jean at all. I've worked hard all

17

these years to give her a better chance than I had and all I seem to have actually given her is a complex!"

Personally, I would like to give Jean a few well-placed swats with a hairbrush, but it's a little late for that.

Oddly enough, George Washington managed to forge ahead in the world in spite of the handicap of having well-born, well-to-do parents. He never whined about the complexes they may have bequeathed him. Abraham Lincoln, on the other hand, came from a background of frontier scarcity and hard manual labor, but he was able to rise above these disadvantages.

Lincoln felt so strongly about not blaming others that he made this statement in 1864:

"I am responsible—to the American people, to the Christian world, to history, and, on my final account, to God."

This is the bravest avowal any human being can make. And until we can accept responsibility in the same spirit, before God and man, we have no right to think of ourselves as mature.

One of the easiest—and currently one of the most popular—ways to escape responsibility for our faults is to run to a psychoanalyst, climb onto a couch and have a field day talking about ourselves and how we got the way we are. It is also one of the more expensive luxuries.

If it comforts you to be told that all your troubles stem from a libidinous fixation on your nurse in childhood, an overpossessive mother or an overdemanding father, then go right ahead—if you can afford it. Lean on these psychological crutches the rest of your life. Operation Alibi, for you, has been completed.

Dr. William Kaufman, in his splendid article entitled, "Psychiatry for Psuckers," * sails into the "psycho-quacks" who fatten on the public. The patient, says Dr. Kaufman, who seeks psychiatric help all too often "picks up all sorts of psycho-phoney excuses for his shortcomings and anti-social conduct."

While the comparatively new science of psychiatry has provided impressive-sounding excuses for those who can't face the demands of adult living, human beings always have had this tendency to blame their difficulties on some outside agency.

In the old days it was the stars. "I was born under an unlucky star," or "an unwholesome planet," was a well-worn explanation for trouble or failure in the sixteenth century.

Yet Shakespeare's Cassius, in *Julius Caesar*, makes the bold assertion that "the fault, dear Brutus, is not in our stars, but in ourselves, that we are underlings."

One of the most striking qualities of Jesus, if we accept the gospel accounts of his ministry, was his stern and uncompromising common sense. When people came to him for help and healing, he didn't waste time probing into their subconscious to find out who or what was to blame for their predicament.

"Take up thy bed and walk . . . Go and sin no more . . . Thy sins are forgiven thee."

---

* *Coronet,* March, 1954.

Jesus's attitude made it clear that the important thing was to remake one's life to a better pattern, not to wallow in the depths of self-pity.

The royal children of the Tudor kings of English history enjoyed a peculiar institution known as "the whipping boy." Because it was a treasonable offense to lay violent hands on a prince of the blood, no princeling could be spanked in childhood, no matter how naughty his behavior. So another child was employed, at a salary, to take whatever corporal punishment the prince's guardians and tutors thought their royal charge deserved. The post of whipping boy was much sought after, not only because of the salary but because of the prestige and opportunity for advancement in the royal service.

Officially, the whipping boy has disappeared in the mists of time. But for the immature and childish, the need for a fall guy is a primary urge. If they can't find an individual to blame their mistakes on, they will blame the uncertain times, the insecurity of modern life, the chaotic conditions of the world or some other impressive-sounding situation.

Not long ago, I visited an art exhibition with a friend who prides herself on her knowledge of modern art. I found myself in front of a picture that looked to me as if it had been painted on a dare. In my ignorance, I remarked to my friend, "I've got a three-year-old at home who can do better than this. If this is art, I'm Michelangelo."

Whereupon my friend replied:

"Haven't you any feeling for spiritual torment? This

artist is reflecting the terrible tensions and bewilderment of the Atomic Age!"

Yes, even an incompetent painter can blame his lack of talent on the atomic age.

One thing is certain. If the atomic age is ever to bring hope and fulfillment to mankind instead of death and destruction, it will need strong and mature individuals, people who are willing and able to accept responsibility for themselves and their actions.

And for those who wish to grow up instead of merely growing old, the first rule must be:

> *Be willing to account for yourself and take the consequences. Don't kick the chair!*

DAMN THE HANDICAPS!—
FULL SPEED AHEAD

ONE OF MY FAVORITE PEOPLE is a man named Edward Touhey, who operates a limousine for hire in my neighborhood. Eddie Touhey is a man of varied talents. His mind is receptive and eager. He listens well and talks well. One day, Eddie and I were discussing people who had made great contributions to the world in spite of difficult circumstances, and Eddie asked me, "Ever hear of Nathaniel Bowditch?"

I said I had heard the name Bowditch in connection with navigation.

"That's the man!" said Eddie. "Nathaniel Bowditch. Born in 1773 and lived sixty-five years. After the age of ten, he was largely self-taught—taught himself Latin so that he could read Newton's *Principia*. By the time he was twenty-one, Bowditch was a pretty good mathematician. He took to the sea and studied navigation;

on one voyage, he taught the entire crew, including the ship's cook, to take and calculate lunar observations and plot the daily position of the ship. Later, he wrote a book on navigation that became a classic. Not bad for a fellow without much formal education, was it?"

I endorsed Eddie's opinion that Dr. Bowditch was a chap who didn't know a handicap when he had one. Probably nobody had ever told him that a university education was a first requisite for a scientist, so he just blundered ahead and acquired what education he needed for himself. To Nathaniel Bowditch, who navigated the seven seas, as to Edward Touhey, who navigates city streets, handicap was a word that meant hokum.

It is still much in use, however, by people who wish to evade responsibility for failure. Scores of people will tell you that they are handicapped by lack of a college education; but it's an odds-on bet that, even if they had gone to college, they would have found some other excuse for tripping on their way to first base. The mature individual is so intent on overcoming a handicap that he never thinks of using it as an excuse for failure.

Alexander Graham Bell once complained to his friend, Joseph Henry, head of the Smithsonian Institution in Washington, D.C., that he felt hampered in his work because of a lack of knowledge of electricity. Henry didn't sympathize with Bell or say:

"Too bad, son. Too bad you never had the chance to study up on electricity."

He didn't attempt to make it easier for him by saying that Bell should have had a scholarship or more help from his parents. His only comment to the young man was:

"Get it!"

And Alexander Graham Bell did get it, the knowledge that led him to make one of history's greatest contributions to the science of communication.

Is poverty a handicap, a valid reason for shunning responsibility and throwing in the sponge? Former President Herbert Hoover was the orphaned son of an Iowa blacksmith. Thomas J. Watson, Chairman of the Board of International Business Machines, was once a bookkeeper—without machines—for two dollars a week. Adolph Zukor, the film magnate, opened the first penny arcade while he was a furrier's helper making two dollars a week.

None of these eminently successful men talked about being handicapped by poverty. They were too busy overcoming it to waste time feeling sorry for themselves.

Robert Louis Stevenson, whose physical frailty made him practically an invalid through most of his life, refused to let illness dominate either his life or his work. Sunlight, strength, wholesomeness, the vigor of manhood radiated from his spirit, and the current of this vitality ran through every line he ever wrote. The world of literature is immeasurably the richer because Stevenson refused to surrender to the handicap of illness.

How many of the world's great names have become great in spite of (and sometimes because of) handicaps. Lord Byron had a clubfoot. Julius Caesar was an epileptic. Beethoven became deaf. Napoleon was a half-pint. Mozart was a consumptive. Franklin D. Roosevelt was a victim of polio. Helen Keller was blind and deaf from an early age.

Singer Jane Froman was terribly injured in a plane accident, but she fought her way back to health and stardom. Actress Suzan Ball refused to let a leg amputation keep her from a happy marriage and success in motion pictures before she died.

And, speaking of actresses, what about Sarah Bernhardt, "the Divine Sarah"? Here was an ugly, illegitimate child who was kicked around as a youngster and who well might have been excused for never having risen above her sordid early environment. But Sarah became a great beauty and one of the immortals of the theater.

The tall, handsome son of a close friend of mine has stammered since early childhood. But the boy did exceptionally well in his studies in school, became popular with his friends and progressed successfully through the elementary grades. During this time, the parents enlisted the help of speech therapists and psychiatrists in an effort to end their son's stammering, but all efforts failed.

One afternoon Bobby came home from school with the news that he had been named valedictorian of his graduating class in grammar school. And a few minutes later he was leaping up the stairs to his bedroom to prepare the valedictory address he would be called on to give at the commencement exercises.

The boy's mother and father gave him their advice on the material he had selected for his speech but wisely made no mention whatsoever of the difficulties he might have in delivering it.

The night of graduation came and young Bobby rose from his chair as the spokesman for his class. He stood to his full height, squared his shoulders and began to speak. The audience was rigidly quiet, for there were many there who knew of the boy's difficulty in speaking.

He started slowly, gained confidence and went through a fifteen-minute address without a single stammer or moment's hesitation. At some point in the preparation of his address, the young man had decided that he would rise above his difficulty in speaking. And the applause which thundered through the auditorium was his great reward, the accolade of achievement.

Another story from life belongs here. It concerns a man whose eyes were opened by—of all things—a seeing-eye dog. J. Carleton Griffith, a businessman from Metedeconk, New Jersey, recently was driving his automobile through Morristown when he saw a figure start to cross the street at an intersection. When he saw that the figure was a young blind woman accompanied by her seeing-eye dog, he slammed on his brakes, although the intersection was well ahead.

He was surprised a moment later when a man walked up to his car, explained that he was the young woman's instructor and said:

"Please don't stop your car that way again. The dog is trained to avoid traffic here in Morristown and, if all motorists stop their cars, the dog may think this is a normal condition and expect it. If that happens, a blind person will be killed some day by a car which doesn't stop."

I was deeply impressed by the story, not only by the logic of the instructor's words but by the knowledge that persons without sight are moving forward today with the help of these marvelous animals to lead a normal life, to walk in traffic, to go to their jobs.

Here are people who are refusing to lean on the crutch of a handicap. They are mature people, accepting responsibility for themselves in a world of darkness. No life of panhandling and tin cups for them, no despair, no excuses.

Roy L. Smith once wrote an inspiring story, a biography of a man which he entitled: "A Full Life—at Death's Door." * It was the story of Elmer Helms who, at his birth in Huntersville, Ohio, caused a country doctor to say:

"There isn't a chance in the world this baby can live."

But Elmer Helms did live, despite serious injury to his right side and virtually uninterrupted pain that tortured his body for ninety years. Because he couldn't do heavy work, he turned to reading. In 1891, at the age of twenty-eight, he became a Methodist minister. Two breakdowns failed to diminish his drive, and he attracted the attention of John S. Huyler, the chocolate manufacturer. Mr. Huyler helped him financially, and in a few months the man who was supposed to die was out of a sanitarium.

Elmer Helms started building churches, raising mis-

* *Guideposts*, February, 1955.

sionary funds, helping colleges and hospitals. The "one-lunged preacher" raised more than three million dollars for the causes he felt were worth while. He "retired" at the age of sixty-nine, then preached more than a thousand times, wrote two books, raised $500,000 for religious and philanthropic causes, served on the boards of twenty institutions and personally contributed $50,000 toward building another church near the University of California.

Elmer Helms never knew the meaning of the word "handicap." All he knew was that he had a life and a purpose for that life. He used that ninety-odd years of life right up to the hilt, and his name will always be a synonym for courage.

In this high-octane era when so much emphasis is placed on youth, many older people feel that they are handicapped by their age. They sometimes feel that they have been put on the shelf or by-passed by the times. I remember a tiny, seventy-four-year-old woman who attended one of our classes in New York City several years ago. She didn't know what to do with the rest of her life.

This woman had been a schoolteacher until that dreaded day when her age made retirement mandatory. Her savings were meager and it was important for her to keep busy, both for her mental and financial well-being. She said that, along with her regular duties as a teacher, she had once made it a practice to go to different schools to tell stories to the kindergarten children, stories which were illustrated by carefully selected slides.

It seemed to me that here was a vital contribution she could make. Why not reactivate her career as storyteller?

With encouragement, this woman became excited and eager to launch her past-seventy career. She realized that age need not be a handicap. On the contrary— she now had even greater capacities than in her younger days, and a wealth of experience which would make her stories even more effective.

On her own initiative, she went to the Ford Foundation, which has done so much to further our nation's culture. She outlined her plan, a wide variety of story-hour programs for kindergarten children. She was talking with "show-me" people who had to be convinced of the worthiness of her suggestion; but they were convinced. The warmth and the drama and appeal of her stories completely sold them.

Today this woman has the enthusiasm and confidence of a teen-ager as she pursues her storytelling rounds, bringing joy to thousands of children. She refused to let her age become a handicap or an excuse for idleness. Instead of saying, "I'm too old to earn a living," she re-evaluated her talents and experience, planned her campaign for putting them to work again and sold her idea on the basis of its merits. She hasn't grown old at seventy-four—she has grown up. What some would have considered a handicap—her age—became for this woman a spur and an incentive.

George Bernard Shaw was impatient of those who complained of being handicapped by circumstances. "People are always blaming their circumstances for what they are," he wrote. "I don't believe in circumstances. The people who get on in this world are the people who look for the circumstances they want, and, if they can't find them, make them."

If the truth be known, everyone can lay claim to some "handicap" or other, if he puts his mind to it. When I was very young, I found cause for distress in the fact that I was taller than most of my schoolmates. It took several years of living to teach me that height, like everything else, could be an advantage or a disadvantage, depending upon my own attitude.

If we have one leg to our neighbor's two; if we are poorer or richer than he; if we are fat, thin, beautiful, ugly, blond, brunette, shy or aggressive; whatever it is that makes us different from our fellows can be our handicap, if we want it that way.

The immature are always ready to regard their individual differences as handicaps and expect special consideration for themselves. The characteristic of the mature mind is recognizing one's own differences and then either accepting or improving on them.

3

FIVE WAYS TO DITCH
DISASTER

Two DAYS AFTER VJ-Day in August, 1945, Mrs. Mary-Alice Brown walked into her home in Ottawa, Canada, and stood listening to the silence of emptiness.

Several years before, her husband had been killed in an automobile accident; then, more recently, her mother who lived with her had passed away. And, finally, the tragedy that Mrs. Brown describes:

"While the bells and whistles were proclaiming that peace had been declared, my only child, Donald, died. With my husband and mother both dead, I was now alone in my home.

"I shall never forget the feeling of emptiness and blankness I experienced as I walked into my home from my child's burial. No place will ever be more empty. I felt myself choked with grief and fear; fear of trying to go on alone and an even greater fear of changing my way of living. And, most of all, fear that I was going insane with grief. It was horrible."

Mrs. Brown went through the next few weeks in a daze of grief, fear and loneliness. She was bitter and confused. She found it difficult to accept what had happened. She says, "Gradually, I realized that time would help to heal my grief, but it was passing so slowly, I knew I must do something to keep me occupied. And so I went to work.

"As the days went by, I found myself becoming interested in life again; becoming interested in my co-workers and friends. One day I woke to the realization that the worst was past and all future changes would be for the better. I had been foolish to 'bash my head against a wall,' refusing to accept what had happened. Time had taught me how to accept what I could not change.

"This was a slow process. It did not happen in a few days or even a few weeks. It came gradually. But the important thing is that it happened.

"Now, as I look back over that period of my life, I feel like the ship that has had a rough crossing but has now sailed into quiet waters."

Some tragedies, like Mrs. Brown's, are too great for human understanding. We can only accept them. When Mrs. Brown forced herself to accept the loss of everyone she loved, she was emotionally prepared for the healing process of time. Her first rebellion and bitterness against fate were like pouring poison in the wounds, making it impossible for nature to do its work.

There is only one way to face the disaster of loss—

accept it. When the fabric of our life is violently torn apart, only the hands of time can knit up the raveled threads, but we must give time a chance. In the first shock of grief, it seems as though all the clocks of the universe have run down and the moment of our suffering will last forever. But we must move forward to fulfill our purpose in life's plan, and, somehow, as we force ourselves to go through the motions of living, the pain grows less. The day finally comes when we can recall happy memories and feel blessed by them instead of hurt. Time is our ally in overcoming disaster only if we keep our hearts free of bitterness and accept the inevitable.

Disaster is not always so final. Sometimes it is merely a catalytic agent which forces us to act, a necessary incentive to improve our condition. It sharpens our wits to get us out of trouble.

To Krishna, a god of the Hindus, is attributed the maxim:

"Not tame and gentle bliss, but disaster, heroically encountered, is man's true happy ending."

Man's nature is often deepened, enriched and made fruitful by "disaster, heroically encountered." It forces us to draw on resources locked deep within us, resources and abilities which might remain dormant forever unless necessity forced us to use them. In the immortal words of Hamlet, to "take action 'gainst a sea of troubles, and, by opposing, end them," is the second way to ditch disaster.

Here is an example of a type of situation which I

call "the disaster of dust." Have you ever seen the dust bowls of the great southwest? Have you ever seen farms destroyed by the unrelenting winds that sandpaper a man's livelihood away from him? Have you ever felt dust, seen dust and swallowed dust day after day after day? This is the story of a man who did, a young man who, at the age of twenty-one, found himself the head of a family living in the dust bowl. Both his parents had died in the uphill fight for survival against wind and drought.

There came a day for this young man when there was nothing left—no harvest to reap, nothing in the barn, nothing to eat—the end of the line. He sat there utterly discouraged, as the eternal dust peppered the shingles of the farmhouse. Suddenly the door opened and his youngest sister, a girl of eight, walked in with a school chum.

"Jimmy," she asked her big brother eagerly, "can I have a dime? We want to buy some cookies at the store and each of us needs a dime."

Jimmy didn't answer for a long time—and for a very good reason. He didn't have a dime. He pushed his lean hands into the pockets of his dungarees and drew them out, empty.

"Honey," he said softly, "I'm sorry. I don't have a dime."

That night, young Jimmy couldn't sleep, because he kept seeing the little girl's disappointed face as she turned away. The incident seemed to sum up his position in life—he didn't even have a dime to give his kid sister! Jimmy had been able to take everything else:

his parents' death, the grinding labor of carving out existence on the farm, the dust that ruined his crops and gritted the very food he ate. But not having a measly dime to give his little sister, who asked for and had so little, was the final disaster that forced Jimmy to throw off the lethargy of discouragement and take action. Some time, in those gray hours before dawn, he made his decision.

Jimmy had always wanted to be a teacher, but when his parents died he felt his place was at home, trying to carry on. The dust had beaten him, as it had beaten his parents. It was time to try something else. So the next day Jimmy walked into town and got himself a job. He borrowed books and studied nights at the farm, after the children were in bed, for the job he really wanted, teaching school. In time, he did become a teacher in the country school, and he earned the respect and admiration of his community.

Disaster—in the form of a little girl asking her big brother for just a dime—forced Jimmy to haul up his socks and slug his way out of difficulty.

Sometimes, intelligent action can even soften the pain of parting from a loved one. This is how it worked out for Mrs. Nellie Covington, of Jackson, Mississippi. Mrs. Covington had just nursed her three children through critical illnesses when her family physician told her that her husband had a serious heart ailment and that he might die at any time.

"I became full of fear and began to worry," Mrs. Covington wrote me. "I couldn't sleep at night. Soon, I had lost fifteen pounds and the doctor told me I was headed for a nervous breakdown. One night when I couldn't sleep, I asked myself what possible good I was doing with my worrying; and in the morning I started planning things to do. My husband, I knew, could make pieces of furniture with his hands. So I told him I wanted a little bedside table and asked him if he would make it. He said he would if I would design it. The next day I gave him my design and he spent several afternoons working on it. I noticed how really happy he looked while working. After that, he made a good many pieces of furniture for friends who had admired my little table.

"My husband and I then grew a vegetable and flower garden. We would go out into the garden, pick the nicest vegetables and send baskets to our friends. We thought of all the little things we could do to lend a helping hand to others. And when we didn't have anything else to do, we would spend hours planning and talking about the orchard of fruit trees we wanted.

"My husband died suddenly one day at one o'clock. It was then I knew that the past year, instead of being filled with the grim strain of impending loss, had been the happiest year of my life. I had faced tragedy and done the best I could to meet it."

Mrs. Covington's heroic courage in meeting disaster head on made her husband's last year of life happy and meaningful, and she was left with beautiful memories of shared activities and love.

One of the surest ways to soften the effects of disaster is to sublimate ourselves in helping others. I know a woman in Wisconsin who is an inspiration to her community because of the way she rose above her personal sorrow to bring comfort to those who also had troubles. This woman's son was a fighter pilot in World War II who was killed in action at the age of twenty-three. Although his mother grieved for him, she did not ask for pity. As she herself expressed it:

"I know mothers who have never known real happiness. Some have spastic children; others have sons who were mentally or physically deformed and could not enter the service of their country. And many women cry their hearts out for children and are unable to have them. I had a wonderful boy for twenty-three happy years, and I will have lovely memories of those years for the rest of my life. So I must be reconciled to God's will and do all I can to help other mothers with sons in the service."

This she did, working tirelessly to bring comfort to parents of sons in the service and to servicemen themselves. She had mastered one of the great lessons in maturity and learned that by putting her thoughts and energies into helping others she had no energy left for dwelling on her own troubles.

Life is not a joy ride of uninterrupted bliss where we live happily forever after. It is a shimmering pattern of lights and shades, heights and depths, sunlight and shadow. Trouble will not pass us by merely because we pull our bedclothes up over our eyes and refuse to face it. It is an integral part of human life and our maturity is bound up in our attitudes toward disaster.

One of the common mistakes of the immature is to retire from the field and sulk in their tents, like Achilles, when things go wrong. Spoiled children refuse to play a game any longer when they see they can't win; the emotionally mature adult keeps on trying even when the odds mount against him.

Here is a story told me by Mayer Simon of Norwich, Connecticut, about a boy who refused to be downed by disaster. Jack, Mr. Simon's college roommate, was a lively lad who was "really gone" on dramatics. In Mr. Simon's words:

"Jack was a dynamo of enthusiasm. He must have had grease paint in his blood. He worked backstage in all the college plays and acted in some of them. He was co-director of the annual variety show, and he played the drums in the band. After he left college, Jack went to a television workshop. Later he became a television producer on a network and with independent concerns. He loved his work and put his heart and soul into it. Jack always seemed to be living life right up to the hilt.

"One day I received a phone call from a friend who told me that Jack was dead. He was the victim of a rare and incurable disease and he had known, even in his college days, that he had only a few years to live, at best. As I thought about Jack's enthusiasm, his laughter and zest and spirit, I realized that he had taught me a great lesson: never quit until the game is called!"

Jack's determination to use all of life while he had it was an inspiration to all who knew his story. He chose the brave, mature way to meet the inevitable.

A student in one of my husband's classes told us about another young man who faced life with the same courage as Jack faced death. This young man's name was Mike.

Mike was only twenty-one in 1948, but he was old enough to fight in the war between Israel and the Arab States. He lost his eyesight in that bloody action. Although he suffered frequent attacks of terrific pain, Mike remained cheerful. He joked with other patients in the military hospital and often gave his cigarettes and candy rations to his buddies.

The doctors worked tirelessly in an effort to restore Mike's eyesight. One morning the chief surgeon walked into Mike's room and said he wanted to talk to him.

"You know, Mike," said the surgeon, "I always like to tell my patients the truth. I can't cheat them. Mike, you will never be able to see again."

There was a moment of terrible silence when time seemed to stop. Then:

"I know, Doc," said Mike softly. "I think I've known it all the time. I want to thank you for all you have done for me."

A few minutes later Mike said to his friend:

"After all, I haven't any reason to despair. Sure, I lost my eyesight; but I can hear well and speak well. My body is strong and I can walk and use my hands perfectly. The way I figure it, the government will help me to learn a profession so I'll be able to earn my living. I'll adapt myself to a new way of life."

That was Mike, the blind soldier with the bright horizons, the man who was so busy counting his blessings he didn't have time to curse his luck. He rated one hundred per cent in that great test of maturity—the way in which we face trouble. All of us have to face that test somewhere along the line: you and I and the man next door.

To the age-old cry of "Why should this happen to me?," there is only one answer: "Why not?"

The gods have no darlings, in this respect. To be human is to undergo some portion of suffering as well as of joy. Life teaches all of us, sooner or later, that all men are blood brothers in the great democracy of suffering. King and beggar, poet and peasant, Judy O'Grady and the Colonel's lady go through the same tortures when faced by grief, loss, trouble, disaster. The young and the immature of any age react with bitterness and resentment because they do not understand that tragedy, like birth, death and taxes, is one of the conditions of living.

Here are the five big ways to help us overcome or rise above disaster:

1. *Accept the inevitable and give time a chance.*
2. *Take action against trouble.*
3. *Concentrate on helping others.*
4. *Use all we have of life while we have it.*
5. *Count our blessings.*

THE FIRST STEP TOWARD MATURITY— RESPONSIBILITY

<u>Don't Kick the Chair</u>. Be willing to account for yourself; don't blame others.

<u>Damn the Handicaps!—Full Speed Ahead</u>. Don't make a handicap an excuse for failure.

<u>Five Ways to Ditch Disaster</u>:

1. *Accept the inevitable; give time a chance.*
2. *Take action against trouble.*
3. *Concentrate on helping others.*
4. *Use all of life while you have it.*
5. *Count your blessings.*

PART **two**

ACTION

IS FOR ADULTS

1

BELIEF IS THE BASIS
FOR ACTION

IF I WERE TO ASK YOU if you believed in America as a land of opportunity, where a man can go as far as his ability and perseverance will take him, the chances are that you would say "yes," a big, resounding YES, with flags flying. Yet, how strongly do you believe this? If you were jobless, flat broke and with no prospective job in sight, would you still believe this brave sentiment? And would you believe it enough to act on it?

Here is the story of a man who did. His name is Leonard A. Trenchard and he lives at 609 Red Road, Independence, Missouri. Mr. Trenchard, in 1928, inherited $100,000 worth of property from his father. In 1938, he was broke. It happened like this:

"My father was both prosperous and generous," writes Mr. Trenchard. "When I was in high school, he let me write checks on his bank account whenever I wanted money. By the time I was attending the University of Illinois, I was pretty handy at signing checks. I was graduated from the university knowing neither the value of money nor how to earn any for myself. All I knew was how to write checks on my father's account.

"This was my preparation for life when my father passed away. He left me rich and extensive lands in the Missouri River bottoms near Lexington, Missouri. I set myself up as a farmer. Then the great depression swept across the country. My first year of farming found me deeply in the red, so I mortgaged a piece of land to pay bills and replenish my checking account. More hard times, and I sold the mortgaged land for practically nothing above what I owed on it. That was the pattern I set for myself. As I needed money, I mortgaged or sold another farm.

"Finally, the day of reckoning came upon me, the day when I realized that I had neither money nor any more property. If I wanted to live, I would have to get a job and go to work—something I had never done in my life. Panic struck me. I couldn't sleep. My old crutch, writing a check, had collapsed under me; I didn't know where to turn.

"Then one night, after one of my usual nightmares, I faced up to my situation. 'The sleigh ride is over, boy,' I told myself. 'You're a man now, so start behaving like one. Grow up! And go to work!'

"I began to think out not only my predicament but my beliefs. I had always paid lip service to the idea that America was a land of equal opportunity for all who were willing to strive for success. Although times were still hard and jobs were scarce, I had a few advantages:

"I had good health, a college education and some business training—plus the experience and knowledge gained from my failures and mistakes. All I now needed was to stop wasting time feeling sorry for myself and get out and go into action.

"I completely reorganized my life and my thinking. It wasn't easy for me to find a job—any kind of job at all. But when discouragement dogged my efforts, I forced myself to replace thoughts of doubt and fear with thoughts of faith—faith in my country as a place where any man with determination can make a place for himself. And this inner belief kept me from giving up.

"My beliefs were justified. I did get a job with the Union Finance Company in Kansas City. I worked there for four happy years. Then I resigned to go back to the land and my first love, farming. This time, things went better. Gradually, as I built up my credit, I extended my operations. I bought and sold farms. I branched out into other ventures. Success attended my efforts beyond all my dreams, but, thanks to my early failures and the lessons they taught me, I was ready for success.

"My lost inheritance I gained back again, but this time I earned it by my own efforts. Even more important, I learned some great truths to pass on to my own two sons, a better heritage for them than money alone.

"I learned that we must believe in something, but that belief is useless if we cannot act on its principles. Faith without work is nothing."

Mr. Trenchard's story is an inspiring example of the maturing process—of an irresponsible, spoiled boy who grew up overnight when he realized that he must not only know what he believed in, but must test out those beliefs in the arena of action. Before this, Mr. Trenchard had run away from reality like a child. His faith in America forced him to face up to reality like a man.

As Dr. John A. Schindler, author of *How to Live 365 Days a Year*, tells us: "Maturity has to be learned." And all too often it has to be learned through heartbreak and hardship.

That's exactly how it was learned by Mrs. Lillian Headley, of 928 Avenue D North, Saskatoon, Saskatchewan, Canada. Mrs. Headley was a happy, average wife and mother whose life rolled merrily along until one terrible day when an automobile in which she was a passenger rolled over into a deep ditch.

It was thought at first that Mrs. Headley's spine was fractured. X rays showed, however, that, although her spine was not fractured, spurs on her vertabrae had been torn from their outside attachments. She was ordered to bed for three weeks. And the doctor had to give Mrs. Headley unpleasant news.

She must be prepared, he said. There was a serious hardening condition of her spine. After about five years, he added, she would be unable to move.

Mrs. Headley says of her experience:

"I was stunned. I had always been gay and active, rarin' to go. I had been brought up to take things in my stride but now, it appeared, there was to be no

48

stride. As my three weeks in bed lengthened into four, five and then six weeks, my courage and optimism melted away. Fear seized me and I could feel myself growing weaker.

"One morning I awoke with my thoughts crystal-clear. Five years is a long time, I told myself. I can do wonders in five years to help my family. With medical care, a contented mind and determination, maybe I can even help my own condition. I just don't believe in giving up without a struggle and I am going to keep going as long as I possibly can. As this belief and determination struck me, I had an immediate urge to hurry up and do something about it. I no longer felt weak and afraid. I struggled out of my bed and started right in living my new life.

"I took as my motto two words and I said them over and over to myself: 'Keep going, keep going, *keep going!*'

"That wonderful morning was five and a half years ago. I was X-rayed recently and my spine looks good for at least another five years. The doctors tell me to keep happy, keep my interest in life and keep moving. That's exactly what I believe in and I expect to do it as long as I can move a muscle."

Mrs. Headley is indeed another inspiring example of the maturity that comes from having a conviction and acting upon that conviction.

Belief by itself, of course, is not enough to make us mature. What is the good of believing that courage is better than cowardice if we turn tail and run when we are put to the test? Principles have no value whatever unless we base our lives and our actions on them.

Sometimes our actions give the lie to what we think we believe. A woman once told me that a salesgirl in a store had given her fifty cents too much change; she was laughing about it. When I asked her if she had explained the mistake and returned the money, she was indignant.

"Of course not!" she snapped, "It was her mistake; let her pay for it. If she had shortchanged me, I would have been the loser."

This woman would have been insulted if anyone had seriously questioned her honesty, but she seemed to regard this petty fraud on an unsuspecting clerk as something to gloat over. In spite of her outward respectability, this shabby action plainly declared that she was fundamentally dishonest.

An accountant once told me of being interviewed for a job in which he would have the handling of large sums of money. The company psychologist interviewed the accountant to get additional data on his character and integrity. One of the questions he asked was: "If you had a chance to slip unseen into a movie you wanted to see without paying for a ticket, would you do so?" The psychologist knew that a man who seized an opportunity to be dishonest in a small matter would have no scruples about stealing on a larger scale if he thought he could get away with it.

What we believe in shows up in what we do. Jesus said: "By their fruits ye shall know them." Yes, it is deeds that count. All the high-sounding philosophy in the world will do us no good if we do not live by it. Our fruits will be bitter and our lives hypocritical.

Once we have strong beliefs and firm convictions, we must act on the basis of those beliefs.

There is a certain successful contractor and builder in Honolulu today who believes in not giving up. He is successful because he believed that firmly enough to do something about it. His name is Paul N. Morihara.

In 1931, Mr. Morihara was making the rounds of architectural and engineering firms looking for a job. He was young and inexperienced and it didn't seem that he was going to be able to get that experience he needed. Everywhere he went, he got the same answer. There was a depression. Nobody was taking on engineers or draftsmen. There was so little work that even experienced men were being laid off.

"I was downhearted," admits Mr. Morihara. "But finally I decided that, if I couldn't get a job, I would try to create one. I borrowed $500 from relatives and set out on my own as a small building contractor.

"Hard sledding? You bet it was. Who wants to entrust his new home to a builder with no experience or reputation behind him? But somehow, I summoned up the determination to hang on like a bulldog and, by sheer dint of persistence, I got a few small jobs from time to time.

"I remember that my first contract was to build a $2500 home. Due to my lack of experience in estimating, I lost $200 on the job. But I was able to make it up on the jobs that followed. I came through this tough period because I believed in not giving up."

No, it isn't faith that lets people down. We are the ones that sell our beliefs short by refusing to act on them and stick by them through thick and thin.

2

ANALYZE BEFORE YOU ACT

"KNOW WHAT YOU'RE DOING and then do it" would be a good slogan for those of us whose natures are too impulsive—with emphasis on the first four words! While the ability to make decisions and act on them is a necessary part of maturity, our direct action should be based on sound judgment and a conscientious grasp of all factors involved in any decision to be made.

"Look before you leap" and "investigate before you invest" are not meant to mire us down in a slough of indecision and hesitancy. They are meant as warnings against hasty, rash actions which are not based on the facts of a given case.

If a doctor operated on an emergency case without first being sure what the trouble was, the results could be disastrous for the patient. True, in such instances direct action is necessary, but the success of that action depends upon the diagnosis which precedes it.

But let's take a less extreme example, such as that of

Mrs. Theodore E. Couse, now living at 119 Fortieth Street, N.W., Albuquerque, New Mexico. Some years ago, Mrs. Couse was troubled about the expenses of maintaining a home for her invalid mother in Brooklyn. An uncle who had been helping out financially called Mrs. Couse and asked if somehow the expense of maintaining the home couldn't be reduced, perhaps by cutting the salaries of the two women who were taking care of the invalid.

This proposal didn't seem to be quite the answer to Mrs. Couse. She told her uncle she would think the problem over and call him back. She appreciated the fact that he was doing a great deal for her mother and she wanted very much to ease his burden.

"I think best on paper," writes Mrs. Couse, "so I got out a big pad and listed Mother's income, both from her securities and from my uncle. Then I listed all her expenses. It didn't take me long to discover that it cost very little to feed and clothe Mother, but it took an enormous amount of money to pay the expenses and upkeep of an eleven-room house that used twenty to twenty-four tons of coal a year, twenty to thirty dollars a month in gas bills, two women to take care of it, plus taxes, insurance and all the rest. When I looked at the figures in black and white, it was obvious the house must go.

"On the other hand, Mother's health was failing and I didn't know if it would be safe to move her. She had always wanted to spend her last days in that house. I was too emotionally involved to think clearly about this, so I sought advice from a doctor who was a friend of our family. He advised me to see a woman who ran a small, private nursing home not three minutes' walk from where we lived.

"This woman was kind and competent and she was able to take care of my mother at a cost well within our budget. So I made my decision. I moved my mother to her home.

"Everything worked out beautifully for all of us. Mother never knew she had been moved and always thought she was at home. It was more convenient for me, as I could now go to see her every day instead of only once a week. She had better care than ever before. The financial problem for my uncle was met. The experience taught me that if I put a problem on paper where I can take a good, clear look at the facts, usually the problem solves itself. It's a system I've used many times since then."

Mrs. Couse's case is clearly one of those in which the success of the action taken depends on the quality of the analysis preceding it. Suppose Mrs. Couse had acted without properly organizing and studying the facts? She might have seriously jeopardized her mother's well-being without doing much to alleviate the financial picture.

The system of putting all the facts on paper and letting them tell their own story is especially helpful when money problems arise. And who in this world doesn't have money problems of one kind or another?

Certainly, young Mr. and Mrs. Jack Germer, of 511 East Monroe Street, Olney, Illinois, had their share. Like many newlyweds, the Germers found themselves dogged by unpaid bills almost before the honeymoon was over. World War II was in progress, Jack was due to enter the Navy and there were all those bills to be paid.

"Finally," said Jack Germer, "my wife and I decided that worrying would get us nowhere, so we sat down and did a little figuring. It added up to this: I owed nearly every merchant in town, not much, individually, but more than I could handle in time to join the Navy with a clean slate. So we decided to do the only honorable thing we could do—contact each of the merchants and offer to pay a little each month.

"Possibly the hardest task I have ever had to do was to face that first merchant and tell him I expected to leave town shortly and would not be able to settle my account. But when I made my proposition of paying a small sum each month, the reception I received was so heartwarming and kind that I felt a great sense of relief. Facing the rest of the merchants was no hardship at all. They were all as understanding and kind as the first one had been. In time, every one of those bills was paid in full. One of the merchants even approached me when I came home after the war and thanked me for keeping my word.

"Actually, sitting down and analyzing the facts of our trouble made it possible for me to reach a decision and act on it. And it was the right decision."

Too many of us fail to do what Jack Germer did— sit down and take a good, square look at a problem which bothers us. Instead, we lie awake nights stewing about it, we put off the moment of decision as long as we can; or, if we can't, we take some hasty or panic-stricken plunge which lands us more deeply into trouble. We do anything to avoid looking the facts in the face, getting more facts about the problem, if necessary, and studying them until we get a clear grasp of our actual position.

My husband once interviewed the late Dean Herbert E. Hawkes, of Columbia College, Columbia University, and, in the course of the interview, he remarked that he was amazed to see that the desk of such a busy man as Dean Hawkes was clear of papers and files.

"Handling the problems of so many students," said my husband, "you must have many decisions to make. Yet you seem calm, unhurried and unworried. How do you manage it?"

"Well," said Dean Hawkes, "it's like this. If I have a decision to make on a certain day, I spend the intervening time gathering all the available data bearing on that decision. I constitute myself a fact-finding committee of one. I don't spend one moment's thought on what my decision will be; I simply study all the facts about the problem. After I have done this, the decision makes itself, simply on the basis of those facts. Simple, isn't it?"

Yes, and obvious, too, but, like many other principles of common sense, badly neglected. This tendency to base our actions on emotion, prejudice, hotheadedness or anything other than analysis of the facts involved is a sure sign of immaturity. It is an extension of a child's desire to act *now*, to run across the street without regard for oncoming automobiles, to go to the beach when it's a hundred degrees in the shade and he's bound to get sunstroke, to completely disregard the facts in favor of impulsive, muddle-headed action.

A woman once confided to me that she was afraid her husband was unfaithful to her. She was wondering whether to charge him with her suspicions or to leave him and go to her mother's with the children.

"What makes you think he's straying off the reservation?" I asked.

"Well," she said, "it's the way he acts. He used to be easy to get along with. Now he's snappish and critical. He says he has to work late and he's too tired to go any place with me anymore. Just a lot of little things. He even forgot our anniversary. He isn't like himself at all!"

It did sound like something was amiss, but I asked her first to get a few definite facts before she went off the deep end and did something rash.

My first suggestion was that she contact her husband's doctor and get him down for a physical checkup. Another was to try to find out if anything was amiss on his job.

It was the very first suggestion which paid off. The doctor discovered that the man was seriously in need of an operation. After surgery, he soon recovered his former good nature and his wife had no further cause for suspicion.

Yet, even with a marriage and the future of an entire family at stake, this woman had been on the verge of hasty, drastic action based on nothing more than suspicion.

The ability to take action is certainly part of the mature mind. But it must be action based on adequate comprehension and knowledge, not just the first action that comes to mind.

TWO WONDERFUL WORDS
THAT CHANGED A LIFE

In 1946, a young chap named G. W. Costello, of 949 Bridge Street, Niagara Falls, Canada, got his discharge from the Canadian Army. He immediately looked for work and obtained a job as a mechanic with the Hydro-Electric Power Commission of Ontario. For eighteen months he worked steadily and happily. Then came a day when the boss told Mr. Costello he had good news for him—he was promoting him to the job of foreman in charge of the heavy diesel equipment at the plant.

"Right then and there," said Mr. Costello, "I started to worry. I had been a happy mechanic, but I was miserable as a foreman. My responsibilities weighed me down. Anxiety was my constant companion, waking or sleeping, at the plant or at my home.

"Then it happened—the big emergency I subconsciously dreaded. I was approaching a gravel pit where four tractors were supposed to be hauling four huge scrapers. Everything seemed unnaturally quiet and I soon found out why. All four of those giant tractors had broken down.

"If I had been worried before, it was nothing to what I was then. My brains felt like they were boiling and bubbling as I went in to the superintendent with the glad news that all four tractors were broken. After blurting it out, I waited for the roof to fall in on me.

"But it didn't. Instead, the superintendent turned to me with a big smile on his face and spoke two words. And if I live to be a thousand, I will never forget those two words. They were:

" 'Fix them!'

"Right then and there, all my worry, fear and anxiety left me, the world turned right side up again and I walked out. I grabbed my tools and went about the job of fixing those tractors. Those two wonderful words, *fix them,* marked a turning point in my life and changed my whole approach to my job. Every day since then I bless that superintendent, as I go about my work with enthusiasm and a firm resolve that, if things get snarled up, I will get busy and unsnarl them instead of going into a tailspin of worry."

Thanks to the sublime common sense of a plant superintendent, G. W. Costello learned that maturity demands of us the ability to take action when action is necessary. Making decisions and carrying them out is a part of adulthood. Certainly, we must study a problem, we must review all its angles, but there comes a time when we must take definite steps to solve it.

Many people are afraid of the responsibility of making a decision, of carrying through a course of action. The fear of being blamed if things go wrong influences them more than the hope of success. So they avoid situations of responsibility whenever they can. And when decision becomes necessary, they retreat into a fog of worry, confusion and doubt. The conflicts and tensions set up by such postponement of necessary action can, and often do, result in mental and physical breakdowns.

Like any other fear, the fear of taking action on a difficult problem can only be licked by plunging in and doing the thing we fear. Those of us who learn this early in life are fortunate.

Theodore G. Steinkamp, of 1123 North Eustis Drive, Indianapolis, Indiana, is one of those lucky ones. He had a father who not only knew the value of positive action but who also knew how to teach it to his son in a way he was not likely to forget. It happened like this:

When young Ted Steinkamp, at the age of twelve, was beaten up by a neighborhood bully, Ted decided it would be healthier to stay indoors and out of harm's way for a while. A few days later, Ted's father, as a reward for his cutting the grass, gave Ted enough money to go to a movie and buy ice cream after the show. Ted took the money but turned down the suggestion of the movie—a treat he ordinarily enjoyed above everything else—for fear of meeting the boy who had beaten him up.

"My father," says Ted Steinkamp, "asked me if I were sick and I mumbled something vague. But the next evening I ventured timidly into the alley to play marbles. Then I saw my enemy—who by this time seemed to me to be as dangerous as Jack Dempsey and Goliath rolled into one—running down the alley toward me. I hightailed it into our garage, breathing hard and scared stiff—and found myself face to face with Dad. He asked me what I thought I was doing and I explained weakly that we were playing hide and seek. At that moment a voice from the alley boomed out:

" 'Come on out, you big sissy.'

"Dad walked away and came back with a heavy leather machine belt about two feet long. Then he told me quietly that it would be either the boy in the alley or a hiding with the machine belt in the garage. I hesitated a moment too long—and the belt crossed my hindquarters with a sting that far surpassed any blow I had received in my fight.

"I shot out of that garage door like a cannon ball and my attack on the lad in the alley had the advantage of a surprise assault. When I hit him the first time, he wasn't prepared, so I warmed up to my work with relish. I mopped up that alley with him.

"The days that followed are some of my happiest boyhood memories as I enjoyed the rewards of valor and regained self-respect. And I learned a valuable truth which has stayed with me through the years—not to run from reality but to face up to it. I learned this from a leather strap and an understanding Dad."

The ability to come to a decision and then act is not only desirable, it is a vital element in our protective equipment. Although life, for most of us, has a way of rocking along in the same old groove most of the time, we have no way of knowing when sudden emergency will arrive. The habit of taking action, of swiftly weighing the possibilities and selecting the best, may mean the difference some day between life or death for ourselves and those who depend upon us.

Such a moment occurred in the life of Al Bishop, who lives at 1701 Overlook Drive, Springfield, Ohio. Mr. Bishop, his wife and three-year-old daughter were driving to Denver to spend the Christmas holidays when snow closed in on them. The cars in front of them on the highway stopped and the Bishops stopped too. They tried to turn back, but the swirling snow had drifted over the roadway behind them. They were stalled in a one-lane tunnel of snow.

"We sat there for an hour and worried," recalled Mr. Bishop. "We worried more in that one hour than we have in all the hours that have passed since. Night was approaching. It was getting colder and the wind was hurling drifts of snow higher and higher around our car. I looked at my wife and baby and I knew that we had to do something if we were to survive.

"I remembered that we had passed a farmhouse about a quarter of a mile down the road. It meant salvation if we could make it. I took my little girl in my arms and we set out through the drifts. It was tough

64

going. I sank in snow up to my hips and every step was agony. But we made it!

"We spent the next twenty-four hours in the four-room farmhouse, which was a haven of safety for thirty-three other stalled motorists besides ourselves. If, after taking in our situation, we had not dared to take action on it, we would all have perished miserably in the snow and cold."

Yes, there are situations which demand something beyond thought and analysis, where nothing but hard-hitting, direct action will serve.

In the third chapter of *Ecclesiastes,* we are told:

> "To everything there is a season, and a time to every purpose under the heaven:
> A time to be born, and a time to die; a time to plant, and a time to pluck up that which is planted;
> A time to kill, and a time to heal; a time to mourn, and a time to dance;
> A time to get, and a time to lose; a time to keep, and a time to cast away;
> A time to love, and a time to hate; a time of war, and a time of peace."

To these beautiful, wise words, perhaps we could add:

"There is a time to meditate and a time to act."

And when our time comes to act, let's quit worrying, quit stalling for time, quit making excuses. Let's simply pull up our socks and go in swinging!

PART II IN A CAPSULE

ACTION IS FOR ADULTS

Belief Is the Basis for Action. Know what you believe and act accordingly.

Analyze Before You Act.

Two Wonderful Words That Changed a Life. When the time for action arrives, don't hesitate.

PART three

THREE GREAT RULES
OF MENTAL HEALTH:
KNOW YOURSELF,
   LIKE YOURSELF,
      BE YOURSELF.

1

THERE'S ONLY ONE
LIKE YOU

My HUSBAND WAS an enthusiastic gardener and he planned and executed a formal rose garden which gave us all much pleasure. One day, as the two of us were admiring our roses, he said to me: "At first glance, all these roses look pretty much alike, don't they? Well, they aren't! If you look closely, you can see that even with those of the same color and species each blossom is different in some way from every other rose. The rate of growth, curl of the petals, evenness of color, each one has some subtle distinction that gives it individuality."

If variety is so abounding in the world of nature, it is even more striking in humanity. In the words of Sir Arthur Keith, famous for his researches on the antiquity of man and at one time President of the British Association for the Advancement of Science: "No two human beings have made, or ever will make, exactly the same journey in life. . . . Every human life is a unique adventure."

Yes, every human life is a unique adventure. And every human being is wonderfully separate and distinct from every other human being, in spite of the fact that we are all made of essentially the same materials.

To achieve the wisdom of maturity it is necessary to perceive and understand this fact. It is the bridge of communication to our fellow man. We cannot reach him or establish any meaningful relation with him until we recognize him as a person, just as we must be aware of ourselves as persons.

Does this sound easy? It gets harder every day. Although we like to think of ourselves as a nation which has abolished class consciousness, we are in fact class-ridden. We have developed a peculiar jargon which reflects our contempt for man as an individual and puts him where we think he belongs—in a statistical column or a survey questionnaire. "The common man," "upper-middle class," "lower-middle class," "mass market," "lower-income group," "man in the street," "white-collar worker," "blue-collar worker," "café society," and the like—all these labels indicate our unwillingness or lack of ability to think of other people as individuals rather than as faceless, anonymous members of a group.

We are classified up to our necks. We have been surveyed on every conceivable phase of our lives. The social researchers who ferret out this information know everything about us: how much coffee we drink; how many of us drive cars and what kind; what radio and

TV programs we listen to; and even how many sexual outlets we have per year and what kind.

Much emphasis is placed on "adjustment," "group integration" and "social mobility." To be able to submerge one's individuality to conform to the dicta of one's group is considered admirable. Rugged individualism is as out of date as the dodo. Small wonder that we often lose all sense of ourselves as individuals and are frightened to death when we think a thought or perform an action that seems out of key with what others are thinking or doing.

Yet people today are literally starved for knowledge of themselves as unique beings, rare and wonderful identities distinct from every other individual. In spite of the pressure of classification, the strain of conformity, each of us, in his secret heart, knows himself to be and wants to be different from his fellows. Our terrible hunger for expressing this separateness, for breaking out of our bonds, sends us to the psychiatrist's couch, the mental institution, alcohol, adultery and drugs in a vain effort to find ourselves by losing ourselves.

What is the remedy? How can we become more aware of ourselves as individuals? How can we attain a more mature self-knowledge? Here are three suggestions:

The first is by getting acquainted with ourselves through solitude and withdrawal. The high-tension lives most of us lead offer little opportunity for self-communion; we must seek out our moments of solitude.

Now, solitude means different things to different people. One man I know tells me that when he wants to meditate he takes long walks on city streets and loses himself in the crowd. "I can think out all my problems this way without distraction," he says.

My husband used to make it a practice to drop into a nearby church for a few moments of quiet whenever he was in New York City. He said it calmed his nerves, refreshed his spirit and clarified his mind.

My own most precious moments of aloneness come when I am in contact with the world of nature. I haven't time for long walks or outdoor activity; but I can walk in my garden or even just glance out my windows from time to time for a look at the nearest tree, or the sky. The fascinating progress of the seasons is a constant miracle and can be enjoyed in a small patch of ground as well as in a vast scenic panorama. It makes me more aware of myself to be attuned to the natural world about me.

Other people prefer a quiet room or physical isolation of some other kind. At any rate, a few moments of solitude every day, unbroken by ringing telephones or other demands, is a requisite for exploring ourselves, our lives, beliefs and actions. The great philosophers and thinkers of the past practiced and preached the value of solitude: Jesus, Buddha, John the Baptist, Descartes, Montaigne, Bunyan and many others found themselves strengthened and inspired for their lives' work by periods of solitude.

A second way to find ourselves is to break through the crust of habit. We bury ourselves alive under layers of habit and boredom until nothing but dynamite or a mighty effort of will can blast us loose. How many people drag themselves wearily through the motions of living every day, dull and uninspired, chained by habit and inertia?

A young woman in Oklahoma, a student in one of our public-speaking classes, told the following story of how she and her husband broke their own chains of habit:

"My husband and I," she said, "were TV illiterates. Every evening we would come home from work, turn on the television set, eat our dinner in front of it and watch it until bedtime. We couldn't visit friends or read or enjoy outings together because we might miss so-and-so's program. If people dropped in to see us, we fidgeted to get back to our interrupted TV. One day I had lunch with some old friends and I was painfully conscious of the fact that I had nothing whatever to contribute to the conversation. I never went anywhere, I never read anything, I never did anything—I was spending the best years of my life in a darkened room watching a gadget.

"I went home and told my husband that if people could break the dope habit, we ought to be able to cure ourselves of overindulgence in television. He agreed with me, and we set about curing ourselves by making an effort to do other things. Both of us enrolled in some adult education classes in the evening. We began to go bowling occasionally, and visit with friends. We even got books from the library and started reading aloud to each other. I'm glad to say we broke away from our addiction. Our work and our marriage have improved.

We are getting a lot more out of life and we are more interesting and valuable to ourselves and to others."

These two people were buried alive under habit. Until they made the effort to dig themselves out, their personalities remained under wraps.

The third method of self-discovery is that of finding out what gives us our deepest satisfactions in life. Psychologist William James best expressed this thought when he wrote to his wife, in 1878: ". . . I have often thought that the best way to define a man's character would be to seek out the particular mental or moral attitude in which, when it came upon him, he felt himself most deeply and intensely active and alive. At such moments there is a voice inside which speaks and says: *'This* is the real me!'"

In other words, excitement brings our real self to the surface, for feeling "most deeply and intensely active and alive" *is* excitement.

It may be the excitement of an idea, the excitement of a personality or of a situation; but whatever form it takes, excitement is a stimulus which causes us to shed boredom, habit and inhibition and be ourselves for all we are worth.

The quality of excitement is the most essential ingredient for success in a given line of work. It is the emotional fuel that spurs us on to put forth our utmost efforts. Sir Edward Victor Appleton, the great physicist and Nobel Prize winner, once made this startling statement: "I rate enthusiasm even ahead of professional skill as a recipe for success in scientific research."

Obviously, Sir Edward was not implying that professional skill was not important in scientific research; he meant that enthusiasm—excitement—spurred a man on to acquire professional skill.

In teaching public speaking for forty-four years, my husband, Dale Carnegie, found that the effectiveness of speech depended upon the degree of excitement felt by the speaker for his subject. Whether a man speaks about the H-bomb, his mother-in-law or the annual rainfall in Ethiopia, his impact on listeners will be in direct proportion to the strength of his feeling for whatever he is talking about.

A personality cannot be changed; it can only be revealed. To find out what we really are, what it is that makes us rare and wonderful and different from everybody else in the world, we must peel off the layers of fear, withdrawal, self-doubt, confusion and habit that grow around and harden over our inner core until we are as hidden from our own knowledge as we are from everyone else's. Excitement is the torch which melts away these acquired layers that smother our real selves, our real personality.

Excitement has many forms. For some, love is the excitement which reveals them to themselves. Those who saw the motion picture *Marty* will remember how love transformed two otherwise drab and lonely people and opened up new worlds to them.

To others, excitement is a certain kind of work or activity or creativeness that sets them tingling. Professor William Lyon Phelps of Yale University wrote an entire book, called *The Excitement of Teaching,* in which he described his delight in his profession.

Danger or crisis provide the necessary excitement which brings other personalities to life. Public disasters such as war, floods or earthquakes always bring forth their quota of heroes, people who reveal themselves and their abilities only when stimulated by the challenge of an unusual situation. On a smaller scale, many older persons living with their children's families and resigned to uselessness suddenly shine forth as towers of strength and efficiency when a family crisis, such as illness, unexpectedly strikes.

Here, then, are three ways in which we may discover our separate and unique distinctness, our individuality:

1. By cultivating moments of solitude each day.
2. By summoning up effort to break through the crust of habit.
3. By excitement and enthusiasm.

The maturing process of the mind is a continuing adventure in self-discovery. We cannot understand others until we first have some understanding of ourselves as individuals. "Know thyself" is the beginning of wisdom, according to Socrates, and knowing that "there's only one like you" is but a modern paraphrase of an ancient truth.

2

LEARN TO LIKE YOURSELF

"A CERTAIN AMOUNT OF SELF-LOVE," writes Dr. Smiley Blanton in his book *Love . . . Or Perish*, "is a normal characteristic of every healthy person. To have a proper regard for oneself is indispensable for all work and achievement."

Dr. Blanton is so right. One of the great commandments for healthy, mature living is "Like yourself." Does this mean smug self-satisfaction? Not at all. It means self-acceptance, a clear-headed, realistic acceptance of ourselves as we are, together with a sense of self-respect and human dignity.

This self-acceptance is referred to by psychologist A. H. Maslow in *Motivation and Personality*, when he says: "The key concepts in the newer dynamic psychology are spontaneity, release, naturalness, self-acceptance, impulse-awareness, gratification."

A mature person does not lie awake nights comparing himself unfavorably to others, worrying because he does not have the confidence of Bill Smith or the aggressiveness and push of Jim Jones. He may criticize his own performance at times, he may be aware of his faults and deficiencies, but he approves of his own basic aims and motivations and he tends to spend his energies improving his weak spots rather than merely deploring them.

He has the same healthy toleration for himself that he tries to have for others; and he can live with himself without anguish.

Is it as important to like ourselves as it is to like others? Psychologists tell us that we can't like others unless we do like ourselves. People who hate everything and everybody, who mistreat and dislike their fellow men are merely expressing their own frustrations and profound self-disgust.

Dr. Arthur T. Jersild, Professor of Education at Teachers College, Columbia University, believes firmly that education should help children and adults to know themselves and to develop healthy attitudes of self-acceptance. His latest book, *When Teachers Face Themselves,* considers the strivings, satisfactions, hopes and heartaches that pervade the teacher's life and work. Self-acceptance is equally important to everyone.

More than half the hospital beds in our nation today are filled with emotionally and mentally ill people who are, quite literally, sick of themselves. And there are many more thousands who need treatment for emotional and mental disturbances. These are the extreme cases of people who have never been able to come to terms with or live with themselves.

I don't propose to analyze here the different factors and pressures which create this unhappy state of things. I suspect that the extremely competitive society we live in, the value we place on material success and prestige and the old treadmill of keeping up with the Joneses have much to do with our soul sickness. And I firmly believe that lack of a strong, sustaining faith in God contributes to emotional disorientation.

Psychologist Robert W. White of Harvard University, in his thought-provoking book *Lives in Progress: A Study of the Natural Growth of Personality*, speaks of the prevalent idea that "it is a person's job to adjust himself to the forces around him." Dr. White goes on to say that this type of thinking has set up as its ideal "the person who all-too-successfully adjusts to narrowing channels, monotonous routines, imposed restrictions, and the pressure to fulfill roles, a course of action that can succeed only at the cost of his power to object, to grow, to improve the roles, to invent, to act as a constructive force—in short, to have any creative front in his development."

I heartily agree with Dr. White. Few of us have the courage to stand alone or the clarity of purpose to know what we stand for. Our behavior is largely dictated by our social and economic group. We dress, eat, live and think pretty much as our neighbors do. And if this environment conflicts with our own individual personality, we often become neurotic and miserable. We feel lost and bewildered; we don't like ourselves.

I recall a student in one of our Carnegie Courses for Women some years ago who was suffering from this type of conflict. She was married to a successful attorney who was ambitious, aggressive and dominating. The couple's social environment was made up of his friends, people much like himself, whose standards of achievement were measured by prestige and outward accomplishment. The wife was a quiet, unassuming person who felt submerged and belittled in this atmosphere. The fine qualities she possessed were overlooked and unappreciated. She became increasingly distrustful of her own competence and distressed because she could not measure up to what she felt was expected of her. She didn't like herself.

This woman's problem was not to adjust to her environment, but to adjust to herself; to accept herself happily for what she was and throw off the strain of wishing to be something entirely different. She needed the confidence that comes from feeling that one has a valid function to perform in life, and knowing that one must perform in terms of one's own personality, not somebody else's.

Her first step toward regaining her own approval was to stop judging herself by the arbitrary standards of others. She had to figure out her own set of values and then start living by them. She also had to learn to be more easygoing with herself and less self-critical.

Excessive faultfinding with themselves is one of the symptoms displayed by people who do not like themselves. Self-criticism, up to a point, is healthy, constructive and necessary to improvement. But when it becomes an obsession it paralyzes us for positive action.

One evening, many years ago, I was with my husband when he was teaching one of his classes. A woman student in the class came up to him afterward and complained about not speaking as well as she thought she should.

"When I get up to speak," she told him, "I am immediately conscious of being awkward and timid. Everybody else in the class seems to have poise and assurance. Just thinking of all my faults discourages me until I can't express what I had in mind."

She went on in some detail, dissecting her weaknesses. When she finished, Dale said something to her that I have never forgotten. It was simply this:

"Forget your faults. It isn't faults that kill a speech. It's lack of virtues."

No, it isn't faults that kill a speech, a personality, or a work of art. Shakespeare's plays are full of historical and geographical errors. Dickens's novels abound in passages of sentimental bathos. Who cares? The works of these great artists glow with a timeless vitality; their virtues are so overpowering that their faults shrink into insignificance. We love our friends because of their virtues—not in spite of their faults.

Progress and self-fulfillment come from concentrating on our good qualities, developing our best traits and leaving our faults behind us, where they belong. We must correct our mistakes and then forget them.

When Jesus was confronted by a physically or morally afflicted person, he didn't make a quiz show out of it by asking them how they got that way. He didn't wallow in morbid sympathy for the conditions which had produced sin or disease. He didn't say, "Why, you poor thing, you never had a chance. Circumstances have always been against you. How did you ever happen to take that first downward step?"

No, Jesus got right to the point: "Thy sins are forgiven thee. Go, and sin no more."

Guilt and inferiority complexes, preoccupation with past mistakes and present faults are not lovable nor desirable states of mind. We cannot respect or like ourselves when we fall into these states any more than we could admire them in somebody else. We must let the dead past bury its dead and go on from there.

In learning to like ourselves, we must develop toleration for our own shortcomings. This does not mean that we should lower our standards, become lazy and shiftless or fail to put forth our best efforts. It does mean that we must understand that nobody, including ourselves, can bat 100 per cent all the time. To expect it of others is unjust; to expect it of ourselves is egotistical folly.

I belonged to an organization some years ago which numbered among its members a woman who was a dyed-in-the-wool perfectionist. She was so overexacting in everything she did that most of her jobs were eventually routed to others. She wouldn't give a simple report without hours of painful research. In making a speech, she always exhausted her subject; she also exhausted her audience. Drop-in guests were never welcome at her home; her parties had to be planned beforehand to the tiniest detail. This woman, through great effort, did manage to achieve a cold, mechanical perfection in whatever she did, but it was at the expense of joy and spontaneity and warmth. She was perfect, a perfect bore.

Demanding constant perfection of ourselves is a form of ruthless egotism. We cannot bear to be only as good as other people; we have to excel, to shine, to be the star in the limelight. Our attention is not on giving ourselves and our talents, doing a job for its own sake; our attention is on outdoing others and putting ourselves on a pedestal of perfection.

Being human, the perfectionist fails as often as the rest of us do, but he cannot tolerate or rise above his own failures and he ends by hating himself.

Not taking ourselves too seriously, being able to relax and laugh at ourselves once in awhile is a condition for learning to like ourselves better.

In a previous chapter, I mentioned the necessity for daily periods of solitude to help us know ourselves. Solitude is also a help in learning to like ourselves. Dr. Leo Bartemeier, medical director of the Seton Psychiatric Institute in Baltimore, Maryland, has written that "it used to be customary for people, after they retired for the night, to spend time meditating on the day's activities. It is still a good method of learning how to get along better with others—and with ourselves."

Until we can tolerate our own company, we cannot expect other people to be overjoyed by our presence. Harry Emerson Fosdick once observed that people who cannot bear to be alone are like "pools forever blown upon by restless winds that never grow calm enough to reflect anything beautiful."

By learning to be alone with ourselves we find an

inner anchorage, a point of reference, a home base for our relations with the world outside. In her beautiful book, *Gift From The Sea*, Anne Morrow Lindbergh writes: "Only when one is connected to one's own core is one connected to others. And for me, the core, the inner spring, can best be found through solitude."

Solitude provides us with perspective from which we can view our lives more objectively. "Be still, and know that I am God," is the advice given us in the *Psalms*. It is still good advice. Solitude is as beneficial to the soul as fresh air is to the body.

To be completely dependent upon others for satisfaction and happiness is to place a burden upon those we love and take the joy out of our relations with them. To like, respect and enjoy ourselves is as much a part of the healthy personality as is the ability to like others.

3

CONFORMITY: REFUGE OF THE FRIGHTENED

"WHOSO WOULD BE A MAN, must be a nonconformist. Nothing is at last sacred but the integrity of your own mind. . . . All the mistakes I make arise from forsaking my own station and trying to see the object from another person's point of view."

These words of that great nonconformist, Ralph Waldo Emerson, will undoubtedly come as a shock to those who believe that "seeing another person's point of view" is the first requirement of good human relations.

Perhaps we might paraphrase Emerson in this way: "By all means, see things from the other person's point of view—but always act upon your own point of view."

If there is one solid benefit to be derived from maturity, surely it is the discovery of our own convictions, and the courage to act upon those convictions regardless of where the chips may fall.

The young and the inexperienced have a terror of being different . . . of not dressing, acting, talking or thinking in the manner acceptable to the particular group to which they belong. Parents of teen-agers are constantly butting their middle-aged heads against this disconcerting fact: "Sally's mother lets her wear lipstick." "All the other kids go out with boys at my age." "For Pete's sake, do you want me to be a freak? Nobody else has to come in at eleven." And so on.

A child must function in the world of his own contemporaries—what his own friends and playmates think of him—and his necessity to be accepted by them is the most important social fact of his existence. The conflict between the standards of this group and the standards his parents wish him to live by constitutes one of the biggest hurdles of adolescence. It is a constant headache to parents and child alike.

When we are feeling our way along in an unfamiliar situation, with no previous experience to guide us, the wisest thing to do is conform to generally accepted standards—until such time as experience and confidence give us strength to live by our own convictions and standards. Only a fool rebels before he knows what he is rebelling against or why he is doing it.

There comes a time, however, when we develop our own system of values. We discover, for instance, that honesty really is the best policy, not merely because we have been taught so by others, but because our own experience or observation or intelligence has proved to us that crime does not pay. Fortunately for society, most of us agree on big basic principles of living, otherwise, we would live in a state of perpetual anarchy.

But even basic principles can sometimes be challenged, and nonconformists are responsible for the advance of civilization. Nobody ever successfully disagreed with the centuries-old dictum that human slavery was necessary and right until a few wild-eyed radicals raised their voices against it. Confession by torture, child labor, cruel and unusual punishment, misrepresentation of products—the list is long of abuses which once were accepted without question by the majority, until a determined minority stubbornly insisted that everybody else was out of step.

Nonconformity is not comfortable. Usually, it isn't pleasant. Sometimes it isn't even safe. Most of us prefer to move placidly along with the herd, protected by the anonymity of numbers, accepting without question or argument the guidance of our various shepherds. We are frightened at the mere thought of doing anything else. What we fail to realize is that this kind of safety is deceptive: nothing is more vulnerable than a herd which can be stampeded in any direction.

The pursuit of conformity, like that of security, ends with slavery. Man finds his true freedom only by accepting life's challenges, throwing himself head on into its struggles, having his passage disputed. In the words of Edgar Ansel Mowrer, the famous war correspondent and author: "Men and women do not achieve integrity by pursuing the negative virtues—adjustment, security, or even conventional happiness. . . . They achieve excellence (and the highest happiness) by accepting burdens. A healthy people thrives under troubles, as our ancestors knew well."

Earlier in this book, I have discussed the necessity of accepting responsibility for oneself as the first requirement of maturity. Coming of age means, in every sense of the word, a passing forth from the shelter of parental protection into the wide-open spaces of adulthood.

If we are truly mature, we will not need to step back into the refuge of the frightened—conformity; we will not need to hide our individuality in the group; we will not need to accept blindly the thinking of others without subjecting it to our own scrutiny.

The man or woman with a mission which dominates his entire life and personality does not need a lecture on the value of standing up for principle against the whole world, if necessary. He is so driven by crusading zeal that he has no choice; a great inner urge drives him relentlessly on in the face of every conceivable obstacle.

But the rest of us—you, I or the man next door—are apt to find that we are often swayed by group pressures simply because we figure that if so many people disagree with us, we must be wrong. Our conviction is smothered by sheer weight of numbers. We lose, or lack confidence, in our own judgment when it is opposed by enough people.

There are those who believe that nonconformity consists of eccentricity or some superficial manifestation of being "different." It does not mark us as free and independent souls to grow a beard, walk barefoot down Main Street, wear a T-shirt to a formal or, if we are female, to smoke cigars at the opera house. It marks us only as immature exhibitionists on the same mental level as the inhabitants of the monkey house at the zoo.

Maturity develops our basic convictions and beliefs, and it imposes on us the necessity of living by them. Every man has an obligation to himself, mankind and God to make the best use of the capabilities he has in whatever way seems best to him and most conducive to human happiness.

I shall always admire Emerson for taking a firm stand in this respect. He was constantly being approached to lend his support to the antislavery and other important movements of his day. He consistently refused on the grounds that he could contribute more to society by doing what he felt was his own particular task, his unique contribution. He sympathized with these reform movements and wished them well, but he could see no point in dissipating his own genius by deflecting its energy to other objects. His attitude was based on principle and he was willing to sacrifice popularity for the sake of that principle.

It takes courage to champion an unpopular cause or to go counter to popular opinion. But there is no braver sight than a nonconformist standing up for his convictions when the chips are down.

I was a guest at a social gathering recently when the conversation turned to a controversial subject currently much in the news. All the guests held the same opinion. All except one man. He politely refrained from entering the discussion until someone asked him point-blank what he thought about it. "I hoped you wouldn't ask me," he smiled, "since I am on the opposite side of the fence from everybody else here and this is a social occasion. But, since you did ask me, this is what I think." And he went on to outline his opinions. He was beset on all sides by argument, but he stanchly defended his position without giving an inch and without a single supporter of his views. He didn't win any converts to his opinions, but he did win respect for sticking to what he believed when it would have been easier for him merely to echo the majority.

It was not too long ago that a person had to act on his own judgment in order to live at all. The pioneers, crossing the plains with the wagon wheels rolling westward, couldn't run to an expert for advice or go along with some fad of the day. In any crisis or emergency, they had only themselves to rely on. Sickness? They had no doctors, so they used home remedies and common sense. An attack by Indians? They had no police force on the prairies, only their own strength and cunning. Shelter for their families? There were no building contractors, just the skill of their bare hands. Food? They had to raise it or forage for it. These people had to make their own decisions on every important issue of their lives. And, on the whole, they managed pretty well.

Today, we live in an age of specialists, and we have become so used to relying on their authoritative opinions that we have gradually lost confidence in our own ability to form an opinion or develop a conviction on any subject. The experts have taken over because we let them. We dropped the ball when we could have gone through left tackle or swept around right end.

Our educational trends today are shot through with preconceived personality patterns. There is much ado, for example, about "training for leadership," in spite of the fact that most of us will be followers, not leaders. We need leadership training, but we also need to be taught how to follow intelligently and thoughtfully, like men, instead of blindly moving with the herd like cattle going to the slaughterhouse.

Our children, according to educator Walter B. Barbe, are being trained to develop surface traits of personality to conform to our national ideal of what constitutes a good personality—gregariousness, popularity, ability to adjust to groups and so on. There is no place, says Mr. Barbe, for the retiring child; withdrawal is a certain sign of emotional maladjustment. Every child must want to play games and be the captain. Every child must have a definite opinion on every topic. Every child must be liked by all the others.

If the happiest and best potential citizens are to emerge from our school system, he reasons, there must be a place for the nonconforming child who likes to read even better than he likes to play baseball, who enjoys music more than he does a football game. Such a child must be permitted to be different without being looked upon as a social misfit.

It is a brave parent who will dare to raise his voice about how and what his children are to be taught in the public schools. He is more apt to be told to leave these matters to the qualified experts in matters educational. Yet, I know a young man in a suburban community who stood up alone to protest the way his sons were being educated. He was a nonconformist, and he had faith in his convictions. He kept asking questions and bucking the tide of popular opinion, with the result that a year later he was elected to his community's board of education. Today, his children and hundreds of others have reaped the benefits of the changes in education which he started that night he stood up alone to face his neighbors at a public meeting.

We have pediatricians who tell us how to feed, rear and care for our children and child psychologists to tell us how to foster proper behavior patterns. Business consultants tell us how to run our businesses. In politics, we rarely vote as individuals but more as members of some particular group. Even our most tender and intimate relationship—our love life—has been invaded by the experts. It is observed, charted and retailed to a public who, upon digesting the results, decides this then must be the gospel for all situations.

It's far past time for men and women to decide that they can be the greatest specialists in the world—for themselves, their families and their businesses. Doing something only because some "expert" has decreed it or because it's fashionable strikes me as so much buncombe.

Edgar Mowrer has written often to warn us of what he calls the "herd State"—the denial of supreme value to the human individual.

"Such a denial," he wrote for the *Saturday Review of*

Literature, "was the kernel of the unlamented Nazi regime. It inspires both the cold inhumanity and the tyranny of the USSR. It is the most 'un-American' of possible societies.

"The United States was originally dedicated to the preservation not only of national independence but of personal pre-eminence within the national state. If, however, the American can be further bullied or educated or bribed into renouncing his individuality, then it becomes hard to explain his hostility to governments based upon mass anonymity."

And as Mr. Mowrer concluded his article: "Because men are still incapable of being angels is no good reason why they should be ants."

Admittedly, one of the hardest commandments we can lay down for ourselves today is "Be yourself." It is difficult to know ourselves, much less *be* ourselves, in a society based upon mass production, mass media, and assembly-line education. We tend to class people according to the particular group thinking they represent: "He's a union man." "She's a corporation wife." "He's a liberal," or "a reactionary." Most of us wear labels ourselves and we hang labels relentlessly on others. We sound like children playing Cops and Robbers.

President Harold W. Dodds of Princeton University was so concerned over the problem of conformity vs. nonconformity that he used "The Importance of Being an Individual" as his topic for the baccalaureate address delivered to the class of 1955 at Princeton in June of that year.

"However heavy may be the pressures urging you to conform here or elsewhere," he told the graduates, "if you have the makings of a genuine individual, you will discover that, no matter how hard you try to rationalize surrender to them, you will not succeed save at the loss of the greatest asset you possess, your self-respect. The divine urge to be an individual, the real man's resistance to being a rubber stamp even if being one pays off in short-term satisfactions, will keep cropping up to disturb your peace of mind."

And President Dodds went on to make the very deep point that man "will find the answer to why he is here on earth, what he should be doing while he is here, and where he is going hereafter only within himself."

Sir Percy Spender, Australian Ambassador to the United States, had this to say on the day he was installed as Honorary Chancellor of Union College and Union University in Schenectady, New York, in June of 1955:

"Life is given to us to use as best our varying talents will permit us. We owe to our country, to our community, to our family special obligations which we have come to accept because we deem them obligations which it is proper we should discharge if our lives are to be lived at all usefully. But subject to these obligations—without which there could be no ordered society within which our talents and individuality could express themselves—we have the right and the glorious opportunity to develop our own separate individualities in the pursuit of happiness not only for ourselves but for those we love, for our fellow men, for mankind in general."

Perhaps what I have tried to say here is best expressed in those memorable words of the Eighth Psalm wherein the psalmist asked the Lord if the individual man were not too minute a particle in space to be of any great significance.

"When I consider thy Heavens, the work of thy fingers,
The moon and the stars which thou has ordained,
What is man, that thou art mindful of him?
And the son of man, that thou visitest him?
For thou hast made him a little lower than the angels,
And hast crowned him with glory and honor.
Thou madest him to have dominion over the works of thy hands;
Thou has put all things under his feet."

Only the mature mind is capable of appreciating this glorious potential of man. Only the mature spirit lives with the proud knowledge that he is "a little lower than the angels" rather than a little higher than the apes. For such a mind and spirit, conformity, that refuge of the frightened, is only a word, not a reality. For he, like Emerson, holds most sacred the integrity of his own mind.

4

WHY IS A BORE?

PEOPLE CAN INSULT other people deliberately. It is easy to do a dirty trick with malice aforethought and, as you have undoubtedly noticed, people do it every day. However, nobody—but nobody—in his right mature mind ever bores another person on purpose.

We all have our special lists of pet peeves, our private hates, but we all agree that the Bore is the greatest business and social menace known to man. The tragic truth is that to date no concerted attempt has been made to eliminate him, outside of merely avoiding him. The law, in its questionable wisdom, has not decreed that boredom is a felony, nor even a misdemeanor, so we can't place the offenders in solitary where they belong. There's no tight little island to which we can deport them. We know how to keep the hoof and mouth disease from our shores but, alas, not the dread ailment called boredom.

Our advertising touts remedies for practically every

malady known to man—athlete's foot, halitosis, constipation, throat scratch, headache, corns and falling hair. But nobody claims he can cure us of boring other people.

If prevention is the best form of cure, then a proper diagnosis of a disease should precede treatment. So let's analyze some of the more acute forms of socially inflicted boredom. And if we find ourselves falling into any of these categories, we can be pretty sure of the reason we didn't get an invitation to Mrs. Rippinghast's last lawn party. Here is the list and any connection with persons living or dead is strictly on purpose:

1. *Talking endlessly about children or grandchildren or your pet subject.*

The simple, polite inquiry: "How are the kids?" is enough to bring on a flood of information from this particular type of bore, none of it worth listening to. You have opened the gates, however, and you must sit there while the flood waters inundate you. If you know the same brand of bore that I do, the answer comes something like this:

"Well, Johnny—you know, he's the youngest one— he simply won't eat his Pablum lately. Just yesterday he took the whole bowl and turned it over on his head. He's such a funny little boy. So, I called up our pediatrician. 'Doctor,' I said, 'I've tried everything and that child either spits out his cereal or throws it on the floor. When he's being especially difficult, he drapes it on himself.'

"He asked me if I had tried mixing it with bananas,

but it's the strangest thing, Johnny has never liked bananas, either. He is so cute about it—'nannies,' he calls them. 'No nannies,' he says, and waves his little fat hands and yells to high heaven. Of course, he is advanced for his age; none of the other youngsters in our neighborhood are so expressive. It's simply amazing! Why, only the other day he pulled the tablecloth off the table and then looked up at me with those beautiful dark eyes of his and said, 'Johnny spill.' His father and I almost died laughing."

Phew! By this time, you are almost dead too, but not of laughing.

A bore of this type has the infernal knack of dragging every conversation, no matter how far removed in subject matter, right back to his own obsession. You can bring up Brando or Bulganin to no avail; he—or she—still wants to talk about Baby.

I know such a woman. If the conversation is running strong on international relations or the high cost of beef, she will, somehow, with diabolical cunning, channel it right back to her daughter Daphne. This is how she does it:

"No, you just can't trust those Russians. Only last summer, one of Daphne's many college friends wanted her to go on a trip to Europe. They weren't actually going behind the Iron Curtain, but they thought about going to West Berlin. Daphne said to me, 'Mother, what do you think about it?' and I said to her . . ."

And so on and on. Actually, boring people are grossly immature people. They are not grown up enough to know the first rule of making friends—consideration of others.

Boredom, unfortunately, isn't generated solely by the ramblings of proud fathers and doting mothers. A salesman, fresh from a successful trip selling snow tires in Buffalo, can wither you with full details of how he conned the department store buyer into a $10,000 order.

And have you ever listened to a bridge player retell the intricacies of that little slam he made—vulnerable and *doubled?* Then, too, there is the movie fan. He likes to tell the plot of the latest whodunnit at such length that you want to hit him with the table lamp.

The sickening sphere of boring topics encompasses many subjects; it doesn't have to be children, bridge or the movies. It can be hubby's hobby of refinishing furniture or Cousin Emma's fruit closet. It can be Brother's job or Cousin Laura's miseries. It can be dogs and cats. I was once trapped on a busy street corner in Manhattan for twenty minutes while an acquaintance treated me to an intimate description of the way her pet canary's intestines were acting up.

2. *Running away from the conversational point in all directions.*

One of Mark Twain's essays is devoted to mimicking a bore who starts out to tell a story and never arrives at the point, something like this:

"Did I ever tell you about my visit to the Hopi Indians out west? Well, we started out on this vacation, see? It was a Friday morning—no, it was on Thursday—you remember, Ella, I told you we'd have to leave on Thursday because I had to see the dentist on Wednesday? My upper plate was a little loose and I wanted him to fix it for me. Gosh, I have the darndest dentist —talks all the time. But he knows his business, yes, sir! I told my boss about him. That boss of mine, he's a card. Incidentally, he depends on me for everything, he's so absent-minded. I was saying to Ella just the other day, 'Ella,' I said, 'what would the boss do if I just up and quit, just like that?' And Ella said, 'Bill, you do that, and I'm going right home to Mother!' What a kidder!"

You never find out about the Hopi Indians—which is probably just as well.

3. *Being a dead pan.*

This type of bore is somewhat rarer than the talkative specimens, which is the only thing to be said in his favor.

You knock yourself out trying to hit on a congenial topic of conversation. You show consuming interest in him. You try, vainly, to "draw him out," and all you get for your pains is a blank expression and an occasional "uh huh." If you're lucky—and I never am—you will be rewarded by "Is that so?" for your one-man performance beyond the call of social duty.

He is Jud-the-dud, a complete and utter blob of insensitivity. Trying to get any intelligent or courteous response out of him is as rewarding as trying to sell stocks and bonds in Moscow. No expression of interest ever disturbs the potato-like placidity of his features. He is a William Steig cartoon come to life—if you can call it life.

4. *Arguing continuously about whatever is being discussed.*

With this type, every item of conversation bounces back and hits you smack in the face like a handball.

This is the guy who knows all the answers to everything and effectively closes out every discussion by a flat statement which brooks no other opinion. Nor does he hesitate to tell you just how cockeyed you are if your views don't happen to coincide with his.

"Man, you're crazy," he bellows. "Don't you know that it's a proven fact that . . ." etc. Or, in his gentler mood he simply states: "No sir, you're entirely wrong about this! Let me tell you something . . ."

The trouble with this juvenile joy-killer is that he is always telling you something—definitely, conclusively, rudely—and it's always something you don't particularly want to hear.

There is only one course of action possible with a character like this: Agree with him, regardless of what he says. Disagree, though ever so mildly, and you will find yourself with a knockdown-dragout fight on your hands. No discussion or exchange of views is possible because all he cares about is expounding his own opinions with the authority of Moses delivering the Law.

5. *Being forever on the down beat.*

These bores operate on the fixed principle that the world is going to hell in a hand basket, that life is a washout, that humanity is composed exclusively of fools, swindlers and no-good bums, that some malevolent destiny is out to get them and even the weather is changing—for the worse.

Fifteen minutes in the society of one of these party pests, and you feel that you, too, could swap hard-luck stories with Job. Because this attitude is, unfortunately, contagious, no matter how sunny your mood you will wind up storm-bound by the congenital crapehanger.

Mrs. X., an acquaintance of mine, is typical. Every time I meet her, she gives me a detailed account of her most recent experiences—none of them, unfortunately, good.

"I've just been shopping," she will whine plaintively, "trying to find some kitchen curtains. And I had to wait all of ten minutes before any of the clerks would even notice me. They weren't that busy, either—just idling about or gossiping in corners. Of course, they took a look at me and decided I wasn't rich enough to deserve any attention. It's the same thing in all the stores. What I've been through lately—and with my health, too! My doctor says he just can't understand how I keep going. My digestion is utterly ruined, and then this weather makes my poor bones ache so. You'd think I would deserve a little consideration from my own family, but that's the last place I expect to find any."

These are only a few of the endless variations on the theme of boring our fellow man.

On and on they go, the gushing girls and the big, strong men. They put themselves in the spotlight, center stage. And the audience reaction is a big, fat yawn and an overpowering desire to be unconscious until the blight passes over.

The insidious thing about the Bore is that, alas, he doesn't know he is one. As we said, nobody ever bores another on purpose. The Bore sees himself as the life of the party, a vivacious cutie, information dispenser, or some other flattering guise. You and I, horrible thought, may be a bore without knowing it.

Fortunately, there are signs and symptoms, which, if heeded, may warn us in time that we are losing our audience.

One is the frozen smile and glassy eye of the listener. When, in the middle of one of our choicest anecdotes about Little Willie, we notice that our listener is looking as though rigor mortis had set in, it's time to stop talking. Of course, this gives him a chance to tell us in detail what his grandchild said to the minister, but then, it serves us right.

Another sign to watch for is a surreptitious glance at a wrist watch. When the watch is shaken and held up to the ear, there is no doubt about it. The curse has come upon us and we know ourselves for what we are. Public speakers are especially sensitive to this watch test, or should be.

The wandering eye is still another tip-off that our conversation is failing to grip. At crowded cocktail parties, when we have a victim nicely trapped in a corner, his only hope of escape lies in frantically appealing with his eyes to each gay passer-by for rescue. It seldom works, because nobody else is going to trade places with this sucker, not if he can help it. In common humanity, we should relent and stop talking.

Some quibbler may ask what boredom has to do with maturity, mental health or lack of it. It is possible, perhaps, to lead the good life, love our families, tithe regularly and make a million dollars while remaining a colossal bore. It is possible, but not probable. Because being boresome indicates a poverty of the intellect, imagination and sensitivity to others that are basic in fulfilling the needs of a healthy personality and achieving a healthy response in others.

The Bore neither knows himself, likes himself or is himself. His basic needs are unknown and unfulfilled, so he has no conception of the basic needs of others in human intercourse or fellowship. He overcompensates for inner emptiness by concentration on trivia, the inconsequential aspects of existence, and builds them up out of all proportion. His communication is as vapid as his mental processes. He isn't really funny—he's a tragic symbol of modern man adrift in a world in which he has no firm anchor or fixed point of reference.

Boresomeness is merely a symptom of personality sickness, of a static personality which has stopped growing.

The maturing, growing individual is able to discuss almost anything without being boring because everything he touches becomes meaningful. The same subjects which come alive and sparkling for him are dull and lifeless when handled by the Bore.

The Bore is perhaps the greatest inducement to us to strive for maturity, because he is such a Horrible Example of what will happen to us if we don't.

5

THE MATURING MIND:
ADVENTURE IN ADULT LIVING

IN FEBRUARY, 1956, the New York *Times* published an interview with a man named Isaac Presler. Mr. Presler, a department-store salesman during the daytime, had just received his high-school diploma after completing four years of night school. He immediately enrolled in night classes at Brooklyn College, planning to complete his college course and then take up the study of law. In his first composition for his freshman English class entitled "What Is Happiness?" Mr. Presler wrote:

"To get your high-school diploma, to start out in college and to look forward to being a lawyer—this is happiness to me.

"Just looking forward gives me joy within," Mr. Presler said. "It will be five years or more of college, depending on how I master it, then another five years at law school."

Sounds like an ambitious program for a young man, doesn't it? Well, Isaac Presler celebrated his sixtieth birthday just before enrolling for his college course. He, like many others, knows that to the mature mind learning is a joyful adventure which may be undertaken at any age.

Nor is education limited to the confines of a high-school or university campus, the formal experience of a set curriculum.

Dr. A. Lawrence Lowell, former president of Harvard University, once wrote that the most any college or system of training could do for us was to help us to help ourselves. He was saying, of course, that in the final analysis we all have to educate ourselves, that education is a process of growth, the expansion and development of the mind through the voluntary use of the mind itself.

Once this is understood, education and self-improvement become thrilling experiences which we may pursue at any stage of our lives. There is no better investment than the development of an intense intellectual passion which will sustain us later in life.

One of the most lovable and fascinating men I have ever met was the father of America's favorite newscaster, Lowell Thomas. Dr. Thomas, Lowell's father, was a highly cultured gentleman. His brilliant, searching mind embraced a wide scope of interests. Dr. Norman Vincent Peale tells of visiting him when Dr. Thomas's life was drawing to its close. Although his physical strength was ebbing, his mind was as keen and versatile as ever. After the first greetings, Dr. Thomas said to Dr. Peale, "Norman, what is your opinion of Henry VIII?"

Somewhat surprised, Dr. Peale confessed that he hadn't given much thought to Henry VIII. Dr. Thomas then told him that he had been studying and thinking about the Tudor monarch lately and he didn't think historians had done him justice. He proceeded to give his own opinion of Henry with all the fervor of intellectual enthusiasm.

Although his body was confined to a sickroom, the mind of Dr. Thomas was alive, vigorous and ranging the centuries until the end.

The mind is the most important and essential part of our make-up. If we nourish and exercise it, it grows. If it is starved and neglected, it becomes stunted and atrophied from lack of use.

Nor is it enough merely to expose the mind to educational influences; it must be used, it must react to these influences. Anyone can subscribe to book clubs, take courses, buy season tickets to the opera and attend lectures with no deeper purpose or result than to be able to contribute small talk at parties. Anyone can acquire a thin layer of culture to be put off or on like Sunday clothes. But, underneath, the mind may remain as unripe and undeveloped as ever.

There is only one valid reason for intellectual activity: to enable the mind to grow. And the mind, like the body, grows only by being used.

Lewis Mumford once described the aims we should strive for in education.

"Now the end of all practical activity is culture," he wrote, "a maturing mind, a ripening character, an increasing sense of mastery and fulfillment, a higher integration of all one's powers in a social personality, a larger capacity for intellectual interests and emotional enjoyments. . . ."

These should be our ultimate goals in every phase of self-improvement.

I well remember a woman who came to see my husband one afternoon. She was seeking advice. Her expression was like that of a collie who had been beaten by Albert Payson Terhune. Her problem? She felt that her husband was losing interest in her. Her husband was a successful executive of wide interests and cultured tastes and his wife admitted that she was finding it more and more difficult to keep pace with him.

She bewailed the fact that she had never had the opportunity to go to college. When the children came along, there never seemed to be time to acquire knowledge of music, art and literature—the things, incidentally, which her husband found absorbing.

"Is it fair for him to be bored with me now," she asked, "just because I can't enter into conversation with him and his intellectual friends?"

My husband asked what she did with her time, now that her children were grown up and married. She explained that she played bridge, went to the movies twice a week and did a little reading, mainly, romantic novels.

It was painfully apparent that the woman had made no effort whatever to extend her interests. She didn't lack opportunity for self-improvement; she lacked energy and desire. She could well have used those hours spent with bridge and Burt Lancaster in the more rewarding pursuits of broadening her interests to keep abreast of an intelligent man.

People, like this woman, who fail to extend their horizons are likely to be left alone in the narrow world they have built for themselves. They will complain that it's too late now, they're too "old." They accept their age as the last stop in the timetable of life and never understand that living is a never-ending series of mental journeys for those who want to learn.

Years ago, colleges were few, far between, expensive and, therefore, available to only a small number of people. Even books were not too easily available, and night schools were unheard of. Today the reverse is true. Education is available to anyone who wants it. There's nothing unique any more about Grandma getting her college degree.

I know of a woman in a small Texas town, the wife of a lawyer, who raised five strapping sons, gave them university and technical training and saw them established as professional and business leaders. After the youngest was graduated from college and working on his first job, this woman, then in her fifties and a grandmother, enrolled in the University of Texas and spent the next four years of her life as a co-ed. She was graduated with honors. Today, in her seventies, she is a widow living alone; but don't waste sympathy on her!

110

Alert, charming, busy in community work, she has more friends and admirers than she knows what to do with and is an inspiration to everybody who comes within her orbit. Her sons and their wives and children adore her and treasure her rare visits. She cultivated her mind and is now enjoying the harvest.

George Gallup, founder of the American Institute of Public Opinion and chairman of the New Jersey Committee on Rhodes Scholarships, believes that "too many people today cease learning when they get a school diploma. To me," continues Mr. Gallup, "it should be a continuous process from birth to death."

All that a college can do for us is to give us a time and a place for study; the rest we must do for ourselves. So, regardless of what our schooling has been, the first step in cultivating our minds, in protecting our later years against boredom and loneliness, is to realize the need for continuing to learn as long as we live.

What next? What can the eager beaver of self-improvement do who can't attend college or even night school?

Very simple—he can read books. Herbert Morrison, distinguished leader of the British Labor Party, tells about "The Best Advice I Ever Had," * when he was a fifteen-year-old grocer's errand boy in London. A street-corner phrenologist gave him a "reading" for a sixpence; then he asked the boy what he read. "Bloods, mostly," said young Morrison, referring to the penny thrillers sold on newsstands, "and novelettes."

---

* *Reader's Digest,* March, 1956.

"Better read trash than nothing," advised the phrenologist, "but you've got too good a head for that. Why not better stuff—history, biography? Read whatever you like—but *develop the habit of serious reading.*"

Mr. Morrison said this advice was the turning point in his life. It revealed to him that although his schooling had stopped with elementary school, he could still educate himself through reading. The fifteen-year-old Herbert Morrison found his way to the library and embarked on a course of serious reading that shaped and made possible his future career in the House of Commons. "I have spent some agreeable hours listening to radio," says Mr. Morrison, "and a few watching television. . . . But I have never heard or seen a program which rivaled the value of an authoritative book."

According to a survey made by the American Institute of Public Opinion, fewer books are read in the United States than in any other major English-speaking democracy. The majority of Americans have not read a book in the last year. Six out of ten adults questioned said that they could not remember reading a book, other than the Bible, within the past year. One out of every four college graduates gave the same answer.

We neglect our minds to this extent in spite of the rich storehouses of knowledge which are available to all. Good books are cheap and plentiful. The doors of public libraries stand open to all. Yet, we deliberately starve our minds or feed them on the thin gruel of the popular press or, on a lower level of nourishment, comic books. Materially, we have the highest standard of living in the world. Intellectually, we are poverty-stricken.

There is very little in the way of human achievement, knowledge or wisdom that is not bound between the covers of a book. Whatever we wish to learn, to know, is quietly waiting for us in some library, bookstore or on a friend's shelf. Through books, we can have personal contact with the greatest minds ever produced. Only through books can we roll back the centuries or peer into the future, ignore the restrictions of time and space and live in a three-dimensional world created by the mind.

In the words of Frank G. Jennings, teacher of education and reading specialist in Bloomfield, New Jersey, Junior High School: "The literary experience . . . is one of the most profound mind-shaping events in the life of man. It kept cultures alive through the campfire storyteller. It makes it possible for Plato and Christ to instruct us from thousands of years away. It joins minds and times together for the better management and control of our universe. It is as abstract as the idea of good. It is as precise and as practical as a door latch. It is the golden road that makes man humane." *

Yes, it's all there in black and white in the great books—the flower of the human spirit, the essence of man's wisdom, hopes and aspirations. If we knew, personally, the great men and women of the ages, we would not know them as well as we can know them through their written words. We can walk with Socrates or dream with Shelley, argue with George Bernard Shaw or laugh with Mark Twain. To commune with

---

* *Saturday Review,* February 4, 1956.

such spirits is what most of us would like heaven to be, but here on earth the experience is ours for the taking if we run, do not walk, to our nearest public library.

The natural limits of human existence confine us to a narrow space in the universe. What is sixty or seventy or even ninety years compared to Time and Eternity? What can we possibly know about Man and his experience on this planet when we are bound to only one century, one lifetime—our own. Without books, and the will to use them, we are inescapably bound to live in one small dimension, the Present.

How did a man think in the Rome of the Twelve Caesars? What was it like in London during the terrible season of Plague when the streets resounded with the grim calls to "Bring out your dead"? We know these things through books that bring us, not cold facts, but living, throbbing human experience—a slice of life.

Even the enigma of modern Russia is more easily understood after reading the novels of Dostoevski, Turgenev and Tolstoi, in which we watch a nation slowly rot from within. The seeds of corruption chronicled by these great artists finally blossomed in the red wrath of revolution. What an exciting background for today is found in the works of these great writers of the past.

H. G. Wells once wrote: "I do not believe in the least that either the body of H. G. Wells or his personality is immortal, but I do believe that the growing processes of thought, knowledge and will of which we are a part go on growing in range and power forever."

All of us would do better to give a bigger proportion of our precious time to those timeless books we call

114

"great." Time winnows out the second-rate books and what remains to us is the golden harvest of man's thought and experience on earth. If we are to properly evaluate our present position in time and the universe, we must know a little about how we got this way.

A book which has entertained several generations of readers is more apt to satisfy than one which has merely been a best seller for six weeks.

Teddy Roosevelt who never liked the heading "Books of the Week," once wrote:

"I would much rather see the heading 'Books of the Year Before Last.' A book of the year before last which is still worth noticing would probably be worth reading, but one only entitled to be called a book of the week had better be tossed into the wastebasket at once."

It will probably take you longer to read *War and Peace* than it will to read the latest novel, but, with all due respect to the merits of the latter, *War and Peace* will enter into your blood and bones and stay with you all your life, as well as entertain you at the time of reading. You will pass it on to your children and grandchildren, and in your old age it will glow with new beauties and values because you have gained maturity and insight. It is not just a book; it is an experience that becomes a part of you forever.

Once you embark upon this voyage of discovery, you will understand what is meant by the "maturing mind." Don't worry about a road map. My own life with books has been planless, haphazard, full of unexpected surprises, but very rewarding. I'm like a traveler who, on his first trip abroad, comes unprepared to the wonders of the Old World and feels the thrill of discovery as he gazes upon the Parthenon or the Pyramids, his delight increased by his unpreparedness.

I have heard some of my friends complain that many classics were forever spoiled for them by enforced study or dull professors in college. I never had that problem. I was too busy going to football games and falling in love in those days for any intellectual revolt. Therefore, I came to the classics innocent and unprejudiced in my riper years. I gave them attention, and they have given me, in turn, whatever direction, development and satisfaction my mind has enjoyed.

Accordingly, I can do nothing less than beat the drums for the reading of great books as a road to self-improvement, intellectual maturity and a fuller, happier life.

I was delighted one day to read in the *Saturday Review of Literature* that Phyllis McGinley shared my excitement at the discovery of the great classics. Wrote Miss McGinley:

"There is something to be said for a bad education. By any standards, mine was deplorable; and I deplored it for years, in private and in public. . . . But, as time goes on, I murmur against it less. I find that even ignorance has its brighter side.

"There is such a thing as a literary landscape; to that, to nearly the whole length and breadth of classic English writing, I came as an astonished stranger. No one who first enters that country on a conducted tour

116

can have any notion of what it is like to travel it alone, on foot, and at his own pace."

Her concluding paragraph, too, bears repeating here because it is so pertinent to self-enlightenment and growing up:

"To have first met Dickens, Austen and Mark Twain when I was capable of giving them the full court curtsy is beatitude enough for any reader. Blessed are the illiterate, for they shall inherit the Word!"

Although the reading of good books is the most important ingredient in my recipe for self-improvement, there are many other exciting ways in which we can expand our horizons. Special interests in fine music, art, theater, social service or politics are examples.

My husband, Dale, many years ago began the study of the life of Abraham Lincoln, and he found it so fascinating that he wrote a biography of Lincoln himself. He said the book never made him any money, but writing it made him a better and happier man.

We can all stimulate our mental powers by throwing away the old crutch that we never had a good education and jumping into the adventure of learning. We can grow old in years, we can lose our friends and our health, but we'll never be too forlorn as long as we have absorbing interests to fill the blank spaces in our hearts. And we will like ourselves a lot better!

THREE GREAT RULES FOR MENTAL HEALTH: KNOW YOURSELF, LIKE YOURSELF, BE YOURSELF.

There's Only One Like You. Learn to know yourself by:

1. *Cultivating moments of solitude.*
2. *Breaking through the habit barrier.*
3. *Developing excitement and enthusiasm.*

Learn to Like Yourself by:

1. *Accepting yourself as you are.*
2. *Correcting your faults, then forgetting them.*
3. *Tolerating your own shortcomings.*
4. *Learning to be alone with yourself.*

Conformity: Refuge of the Frightened. Be yourself by developing your own convictions and standards; then have the courage to live with them.

Why Is a Bore? Develop inner resources to avoid boring yourself and others.

The Maturing Mind: Adventure in Adult Living. Develop your mind through intellectual activity.

PART four

MARRIAGE IS
FOR GROWNUPS

1

HOW TO GET ALONG
WITH WOMEN

"HE THAT HATH A WIFE and children hath given hostages to fortune," wrote Francis Bacon some three hundred years ago. Lord Bacon took a dim view of knuckleheads who, by acquiring a family, stuck out their necks and invited fortune to chop them off.

But at least Lord Bacon hinted at the reckless bravery it takes for a man to get married. The common impression of the dashing, devil-may-care bachelor and the cautious, stodgy husband needs to be revised.

Bachelors are actually far more staid, penny-wise and set in their ways than married men. They take no chances on upsetting their prim little applecarts by a visit to the Marriage License Bureau. They are careful, cagey and hard to catch, as any unmarried female will freely tell you. Instead of diving headlong into the sea of matrimony, they prefer to play around on the beach, dabbling a curious toe into the water occasionally but running back to a safe distance when those big, frightening waves come too close.

The man who gets married has the daring of a Jesse James, the courage of a wounded rhinocerous and a disposition to gamble besides which the man who broke the bank at Monte Carlo was a poor-spirited piker. He bets his life, his future and his bankroll on a woman and on his ability to keep her happy. Hostages to fortune? He not only gives hostages, he spits right in fortune's eye and double-dares her.

All hail to husbands, and may no family ever be without one. The remarks and suggestions in this chapter to the man of the house are offered not in the spirit of criticism but on the premise that any man with enterprise enough to get married in the first place should be glad of a few hints on improving his odds for living happily ever after.

Dr. Leonard S. Cottrell, dean of Arts and Sciences College of Cornell University, once gave his blueprint for a good marriage in the following terms: "Happiness in marriage," he said, "is today dependent on psychologically mature personalities who have an understanding of themselves and their relation to other people, and who have a sense of responsibility for contributing their share to the welfare and happiness of others." Dean Cottrell said further that families were being held together "through satisfaction from inner values like affection and companionship, values that can't be forced."

These inner values referred to by Dean Cottrell cannot be forced, but they can be developed, tended and deepened. How? Here is a suggested seven-point program we might call the Facts of Wives, or how to get along with a woman after you marry her:

1. *Give her appreciation.*

If you must skimp somewhere, don't short-ration your wife on sugar. She will work and slave for you, stand by when you lose your job, your hair and your waistline, and wear her old coat one more season without complaining if you never stop telling her she's wonderful. It's amazing how many of our brightest boys do not understand this fundamental female craving. They reason that they married the girl and that fact alone should be compliment enough to last her the rest of her life. It never dawns on them that wives, daffy dames that we are, need constant reassurance that we are clicking. It's easy for a man to know where he stands in his world. If he falls down on the job, his superiors soon let him know about it. When he pulls off a big deal, he gets a raise or a bonus or at least some commendation from the brass in the front office.

The girl behind the welcome mat at home has no way of knowing how she stacks up unless she's told by the man in her life. His appreciation is her only reward.

Look around at the happiest husbands you know, the ones who enjoy homes full of comfort, good food, affection and fun, presided over by an adoring wife. These lucky lads have learned that the best, surest and never-failing way, not only to win a woman, but to keep her intent on pleasing them forever, is to give her unstinted, full hearted appreciation.

One of my good friends is Robert H. Prall, feature writer for the New York *World-Telegram* and co-author of *The Big Fix*, that courageous exposé of big city corruption. Bob is the envy of many a man because he is married to the kind of girl most men just dream about. His saucy little blond wife, Jane, thinks he's the greatest and doesn't care who knows it.

Bob knows how to keep her feeling that way. When his publishers presented him with a special presentation copy of his book, bound in hand-tooled leather, Bob lost no time taking pen in hand and inscribing it: "To Jane, for being my wife—and my life." That kind of autograph means more to a woman than the same autograph on a check. It is tangible evidence that she has been a glittering success in her life work.

2. *Be generous and considerate.*

For some reason, men seem to feel that generosity with women consists only of paying her bills without comment and perhaps giving the little dear a handout now and then. Well, boys, I have good news for you: the kind of generosity a woman sets store by has only incidental connection with money. It's the kind of generosity that says, "Of course, dear, invite your mother to visit us; we'll give her a wonderful time." It's the sort of consideration that prompts a man to pay attention to his wife in public and show her the same courtesy he would a beautiful stranger. It's the generosity that motivates him to give of himself.

Did you ever play the game, in a restaurant, of guessing which couples were married? Try it some time. The silent pair consisting of a male absorbed in his filet mignon with eyes for no one but the waiter and the bored female companion who toys drearily with her food give the impression of having won each other in a raffle. Whereas the man who seats his lady as carefully as though she were made of glass and then proceeds to entertain her with his choicest anecdotes is obviously either courting or dining a lady buyer.

I well remember attending a reception for a man of fame and distinction. How charming he was to everybody—to everybody except his wife. Never once, by look or reference, did he so much as acknowledge her presence. She was at the mercy of strangers, to be accepted or ignored, while her ever-loving husband basked and beamed in the glory of his own importance. A little of the charm he bestowed so lavishly on others would not have harmed his public relations, and it would certainly have gone a long way in improving his private relations with his wife. It was no surprise to anybody to learn that that marriage eventually dissolved into a divorce statistic.

Consideration, kindness and good manners, like charity, begin at home.

3. *Don't let yourself go to seed.*

There seems to be a popular notion that keeping attractive and well groomed applies only to women. We are warned against going to bed in cold cream and pin curls; we are subject to endless pressure to avoid B.O., dishpan hands, overweight and frowsiness. Part of the average woman's obsession to look young and stay slim is born of the fear that if she loses her freshness she will also lose her husband.

But what about the man who comes to dinner every night and runs for the eight-fifteen every morning? While he may be a Brooks Brothers model on the job, he all too often resembles an unmade bed at home. Week ends are apt to find him relaxing comfortably in his T-shirt behind the Sunday papers, flopping around in slippers that the dog wouldn't even chew, unbathed, unshaven and serene in the illusion that he is a desirable hunk of man and his wife is lucky to get him.

This may come as a surprise to these sloppy joes, but wives, too, are attracted by cleanliness and good grooming. We love you as much in your dungarees as we do in your dinner jacket, but we would like for you to bathe, shave and be reasonably easy on our eyes (and other senses) even when you are loafing around the house.

Appearance does not make the man, but it certainly makes up all of what we see of him. Here is a simple check list for the fellow who wants to please the girls, including his wife:

a. Get a haircut before you need one, not after.

b. Never be seen in broad daylight without being shaved, unless you are fishing with the boys at Moosehead Lake.

c. Always look, smell and be clean. Do not suppose that deodorants are for the exclusive use of women.

d. Keep a crease in your trousers. The first sign of a

decadent male is when the crease in his pants starts to fade away.

e. Keep your shoes shined, your socks hoisted on high and your face pleasant.

4. *Understand a woman's work.*

Most women today have a realistic idea of what it means to earn a living. So many of us have worked ourselves, either before or after marriage, that we understand something of the pressures and demands of Madison Avenue or Main Street.

A man needs also to understand the demands of a woman's domestic world, hemmed in as it usually is by the supermarket and the laundromat. It is important for him to know that his wife's environment is more limited than his, that her day is as busy and demanding as his, dealing as she does with chest colds, plumbers and spring cleaning.

A husband should have some idea of what is involved in the routine, sometimes monotonous detail of operating a household, the endless cooking, cleaning, washing, ironing, meal-planning and grocery-shopping. Besides this, a wife must care for the children's needs, do odd jobs like chauffeuring the family and nursing them when they are sick and plan home entertaining. She is often overworked and understaffed. Her sole incentives and rewards are the welfare and approval of her family.

A wife needs some stimulation of outside contact to keep her from feeling that her work is monotonous and boring; and she must depend on her husband to see that she gets out once in a while to see how the other half lives. The nature of a man's employment brings him into the arena of the world's activity, so that he often requires peace and quiet in his leisure hours. It is up to him to strike a reasonable balance between his own needs and those of his wife for a more stimulating social life.

5. *Back up your wife—be dependable.*

A friend of mine was telling about a minor crisis in her life that developed when her favorite Aunt came for her first visit to the family. The lady had no more than unpacked when my friend's child folded up with a bronchial ailment. All plans for entertainment of the guest went out the window, as the hostess was confined to the child's sickroom. "I don't know what I would have done," she told me, "if it hadn't been for Tom. He took Aunt Grace out every single evening and gave her a real whirl. He took her sightseeing on the week end. She had the time of her life and it eased the strain for me. Tom may have his faults, but I can always depend on him in an emergency."

When trouble comes, a husband who lets us know that the Marines have landed is better than all the romantic heroes of fiction rolled into one. And a husband should back his wife up, not only in the big occasional crisis, but in the small events of everyday.

A wife needs his approval and encouragement in her activities as PTA president or chairman of the women's club; in trying out for the church choir or taking a course in dressmaking.

She needs him to back her up when she disciplines the children.

She needs to be proud of him socially. She wants him to have fun, but she depends on him not to make a fool of himself.

She wants the emotional security of knowing that he stands beside her, in small crisis or large emergency, no matter what happens.

6. *Share her interests.*

Success in marriage is largely dependent on the ability to share and cooperate. "You" and "I" must be changed to "we" whenever a domestic situation has to be resolved. Where shall we spend our vacation? Shall we buy new slip covers for the living room or a television set? These are only some of the decisions that must be made. And the more understanding husbands and wives have of each other's separate roles, the easier it is to make these decisions in a fair and friendly spirit.

A man may think it beneath his dignity to show interest in frothy feminine pursuits like clothes, housekeeping and cooking. But, if he wants to keep those home fires of affection burning, he had better come out from behind those stock-market reports and get with it. He expects his wife's eyes to light up with interest when he tells her what he said to the sales manager. Why not show her the same attention when she describes the wonderful bargain she got at the white sale today?

That discerning writer, André Maurois, advises men who want to get along with women to "show interest in what to them is important—the way they dress, their efforts to improve the home, their minute analyses of feelings and characters. . . . When you have time, go shopping with your wife. . . . Give her your advice. . . . Take an interest in the small incidents of which her life is made—the experiences of the children, her clubs, her friends. If she loves music, or paintings, or books, make an effort to understand her tastes. You will be surprised to see how soon you will become interested yourself."

7. *Love that wife!*

"A woman who is loved always has success," says writer Vicki Baum. Being loved constitutes success for a woman. It is up to a husband to give his wife this assurance, not by merely putting a wedding ring on her finger, but by letting her know every day of her life that he's glad he did. "A man likes to feel that he is loved," writes Myrtle Reed; "a woman likes to be told."

For some reason, many husbands feel embarrassed by the thought of saying, "I love you," to their wives once the honeymoon is well over. Well, boys, relax. You don't have to talk like the Continental to impress the girl you married. Wives are perceptive enough to read your affection in a thousand wordless ways: your eyes meeting hers across a roomful of people; a squeeze of the hand at the movies; an unexpected caress. Tenderness isn't mushiness.

But many a woman who was ardently wooed before marriage is bewildered by the same man's reluctance to show his love after marriage. Here on my desk is a letter from a young man named Jack F. Tummon, 101 Edgecroft Road, Toronto, Ontario, who admits that he made that mistake.

Mr. Tummon tells about the care and precision he used in choosing a wife, a beautiful girl who was his ideal of feminine perfection. And, having married her, he confesses that he went blithely about his business, leaving the full responsibility of the marriage to his wife.

Naturally, it didn't work out. The first five years of their married life were an unhappy failure. Then one day, after an argument with his wife, Jack Tummon heard his little four-year-old son saying to him, "Daddy, don't you like Mommy? I think she's pretty nice." Jack Tummon says that he suddenly felt like a Grade-A heel. "I realized that I loved 'Mommy' with all my heart and soul," he says, "for what she was and for what she had done for me. Our little boy was a healthy, pleasant child because of her efforts, not mine. I had evaded my duties as both father and husband. I deserved to lose my family, but I decided to try to make amends. I went to my wife and asked her to help me become a better husband and a better father. Bless her, she did. We have a real marriage now, built on mutual love and respect. We have a new baby girl and a million dollars' worth of happiness. No child of mine will ever have to ask me again if I like Mommy!"

Loving a woman is a lot more than gushy sentiment.

It embraces all the qualities of perceptiveness, courtesy, sensitivity and respect. Many a man hides his deficiencies in love behind the moth-eaten myth of what's-the-use-of-trying-nobody-can-ever-understand-a-woman. These fellows prefer to believe that, while men operate on DC, women operate on AC and it's hopeless to try to come to terms with the critters. They prefer to believe this because it saves them the trouble of trying. Let me inform these gentlemen here and now that women are not strangers from outer space doing business on another wave length. We may be women, but we are also people, and it is not beyond the capacity of man to pluck out the heart of our mystery. Lots of them understand us, even when we are their wives.

But, if you aim to understand your wife, you had better begin by loving her and letting her know it. Otherwise, marriage won't be much fun for either of you.

The American woman, whatever her faults, cannot be accused of complacency. She is so eager to improve herself that she has created a market for a vast flood of information and advice. Among other things, she is told: how to attract men, how to get a husband, what to do with him after she gets him, how to bring up her children, how to keep house more efficiently, and what to do with her spare time—if the poor thing has ten minutes left to herself after all this activity. She attends lectures, she supports countless publications aimed at instructing her in every area of her life, she takes courses in self-improvement of all kinds and she is the target for ninety per cent of the advertising for every known product.

Her husband, on the other hand, is eager for self-improvement mainly insofar as it will improve his earning capacity, make him more competent in the competitive struggle for a better job, turn him into a Man of Distinction. So far as his domestic relations are concerned, he is pretty well pleased with himself as he is. How many books or magazine articles or lecture courses do you see on the subject of how to be a better husband and father or how to attract a wife and hold her affection? Improving marriage relations is left to the little woman. So far as adjusting to the personality of one's marriage partner is concerned, let Georgette do it seems to be the male motto.

Men are quick to explain to us that they are still the family breadwinners and must concentrate their energies on job improvement rather than husband improvement. But men, women and marriages do not live by bread alone. Being a good provider and staying on speaking terms with the finance company are only the beginning, not the be-all and end-all of masculine responsibility.

Several years ago, President Lynn White of Mills College wrote an excellent book called *Educating Our Daughters*, in which he criticized colleges for educating women exactly as though they were men. He maintained that women should have a basic curriculum tailored realistically to fundamental feminine needs. Women should be educated, he said, with the thought in mind that most of them will be wives and mothers.

So far, so good. But it still isn't the answer to how to achieve a happy marriage. What is the use of educating our daughters to be good wives and mothers only to see them marry men who, however expert they may be in earning a living, are bumbling amateurs as husbands and fathers? Why not a little training in this important area of human experience for the men our daughters are going to marry?

The great French novelist, Honoré de Balzac, once wrote that "the majority of husbands remind me of an orangoutang trying to play the violin."

The realization that marriage is a man's job as well as a woman's might make these husbands seem less like orangoutangs and more like Fritz Kreislers.

From the beginning of time, the home has been a basic human institution. It holds the promise of the future as well as the reality of the present. It protects, nurtures and indoctrinates mankind. Wars have been fought from it and for it. It is the sacred citadel.

Why should the preservation of anything so vital to the human race be relegated exclusively to one sex? The fact that women spend more hours in the home than do men doesn't mean that men need homes less than women.

Home is not only a place in which to live, eat, sleep and rear children. It is all this, plus; and the plus gives it significance and value. This plus quality is composed of warm, human elements of shared love, laughter, tears, joy and sorrow. A woman can't supply all this alone; it must be created by two people.

I suggest humbly, therefore, that our men give us a break by giving more attention to their own specific roles as husbands and fathers, at least a proportionate amount of the intelligent thought and energy they give to improving themselves as business leaders.

"Marriage is a searching test of our maturity as persons," writes David R. Mace, Chairman of the International Commission on Marriage Guidance and Professor of Human Relations at Drew University. "Anyone can live alone—there is no need to consider others. It is the capacity to live at close quarters with someone else . . . that marks the mature person. Marriage will either make us mature or bring to us the bitter fruits of our immaturity."

FATHER, COME HOME

AT A RECENT CLOSED MEETING of a board of education in a suburban community, the members were confronted with a boy of sixteen who had been expelled from high school for truancy. His grades were all extremely low, and he was failing in two subjects.

The boy, his mother and father were brought into the board room for questioning. The boy was a nice-looking young man, although he wore the hangdog, resentful look of a youngster in trouble. The mother, nervous and embarrassed, tried to explain that she had done her best to keep her son in line. The father, a well-dressed business man in his fifties, remained silent until a board member directed the interrogation to him. What were his relations with his son?

The father explained that he was a very, very busy man, that his work took all of his time. "I let my wife take care of the children," he said, "and besides, it's up to you school people to see that my boy does his work and gets passing marks."

The school board members—every one a father himself—pressed their questions. Had he seen the boy's report card and done anything about it? The father admitted he had seen it and that he had called the school principal about it. "But," he added, "the line was busy, so I didn't bother to call back."

When the family left the hearing, the school authorities decided to give the boy a second chance. It was clear, they felt, where the fault lay and perhaps the boy would react favorably to another chance.

Unfortunately, it was too late. The boy had formed bad habits he couldn't break without more parental guidance than he was getting, and a short time later he was expelled. Worse still, the father never really understood what he had done—or, rather, what he hadn't done—to contribute to his son's failure.

This isn't the case of a young delinquent arrested for robbery or murder. This is just a mild account of a father who was too busy to care whether or not his son attended school regularly.

The saddest thing about the story is that it happens so often. Too many of our children are growing up fatherless. Oh, they have fathers, all right, in the sense that a man lives in their home who goes by that name. But they don't see or have much to do with him. Father leaves early every morning and he gets home late. Sometimes he works overtime on his job; sometimes he brings a brief case full of work home with him. When he doesn't do that, he is too bushed by his day of conquering commerce to do more than sink into his chair and hide behind the evening paper until the kids are safely abed. His leisure hours rarely include his children, but are spent rather in bowling with the company team, week-end golf, cocktail parties with customers.

Women have been subjected to a torrent of criticism for leaving their homes and children for the sake of jobs and careers. It has been rightly pointed out to them that no job, however glamorous and well paid, is worth the price of unloved, neglected children.

But few barbs of criticism have been leveled at the absentee father. So long as he continues to uphold and upgrade the family standard of living, his moral and emotional responsibility toward his children is seldom questioned. The man who rejects his fatherhood in every way except that of financial maintenance is so much a part of our sociological picture that he is taken for granted.

I once interviewed a man who held a high executive position in a big organization. He was generous in attributing much of the credit for his success to his wife. He told me what an attractive home she had made for him, how she lessened the tensions of his job by the peaceful, relaxing home atmosphere she created, how competently she entertained his friends and associates. He spoke proudly of his two sons, and I told him that I thought he himself must have had much to do with their fine records in school and in the armed services.

"No," he said, "raising the children was my wife's

business. I never interfered in any way. I paid for their bringing up and education, that's all."

This successful, respected man saw nothing embarrassing in admitting that he considered his sons' upbringing to be none of his business, nor that they had turned out well in spite of him. Such indifference in a mother would be considered monstrous.

If physical care were all a child needed, nobody would need a father, or a mother either. But since there are emotional needs to be met as well, fathers are necessary, just as are mothers.

Dr. Richard E. Wolf, Director of the Pediatric Psychiatry Clinic, University of Cincinnati School of Medicine, defines the function of fatherhood in this way:

"A child needs both father and mother, and he needs them to be different. To a boy and girl a father represents a man's strength and wisdom, his knowledge of the world and its workings, his judgment based on experience outside the home. They need to hear his voice in family decisions as well as their mother's. They need to see in him the protector and provider for mother and children. From him they take their model of manhood, and from him they learn an attitude toward women. If mothers do all the managing while fathers sit by, both girls and boys may suffer a confusion about their own status which will handicap them in their relationships as they grow up."

In the old days, before the Industrial Revolution, husbands, wives and children worked together at home as a family unit. Shops were actually in the home itself.

On the farms, the man labored in the fields usually in sight of his family.

There was a physical closeness that is lost in today's urban society. Most men see less of their wives and children than they do of their fellow employees. They cannot always extend the amount of time they have to spend at home, but they can determine the quality of the time that is spent. A father sometimes tries to compensate by taking the kids to the ball game on a week end, when actually he is tired out, bored or resentful at giving up his golf. This isn't much fun for anybody. Dr. Benjamin Spock, famous author of *The Common Sense Book of Baby and Child Care*, says that fifteen minutes a day of a father's kindly, undivided attention is better than a whole day spent crossly at the zoo.

Because a father's time with his children is necessarily more limited than a mother's, the way in which those precious moments are spent is even more significant. They should not be regarded as a burdensome duty, but as opportunities to build a relationship that will grow more meaningful to both parent and child through the years.

A wife can help a man become a better father to some extent. She can handle disciplinary problems that crop up during the day, without saving them up to dump in father's lap when he comes home. She can speak of him and to him with love and respect; children are influenced by their mother's attitude to their father. She can cultivate friends with children the same age and promote more family get-togethers. She can arrange picnics and family excursions of various kinds in an effort to have her husband take a genuine interest in the pleasure and development of his children.

I know a family whose entire relationship was changed by an overnight camping trip. The son, who was twelve, and the daughter, ten, had been badgering their father for weeks to take them camping. And Pop, with a daily diet of nine-to-five accounting, was always too busy, or too tired. Actually, it was the mother who did the trick. She snooped around, borrowed a tent and did a real workmanlike job of rounding up road maps and information on campsites.

Trapped, the father agreed to make the trip and, with a last woeful look at the homework he'd planned to do that week end, set out for the woods. Mother stayed at home, waiting and wondering.

The following evening they were back, three dirty, bedraggled but deliriously happy people. They bubbled over with stories of the fun they had, the lake they had found, the mosquitoes, the time the tent blew down and those scrambled eggs "which Pop fried."

Did it end there? This was just the beginning. This family—Mother's included now—has been spending its summers in a rustic cottage near the spot where Pop and the kids camped that one night. They have a boat and water skis and Pop comes out week ends from New York to share their fun—without his brief case. The man who was too busy to have fun and enjoy his children suddenly grew up to what it means to be a father—but it took Mom's planning and some forest-fried eggs to do the trick.

It is time we overhauled our immature, split-level

concept of parenthood and changed "your job" and "my job" to "our job." Certainly there is a difference in the functions of mother and father, but their ultimate goals and present satisfactions should be the same. Each has a different part to play in a child's development and rearing; but, if either parent fails to assume his responsibility, the whole family relationship is thrown out of focus.

Good fathers generally are good husbands. David R. Mace, author of *Marriage—The Art of Lasting Love,* says that when his first baby daughter was born he was inspired to write the following lines:

> "Two loves have I,
>   And, strange though it may be,
>   The more I love the second,
>   The more the first loves me!"

How true that is. Nothing endears a man to a woman like the look on the face of her child when he runs to the door to greet Daddy.

What are the special contributions a father can make to his child's development? Dr. Gunnar Dybwad, the able director of the Child Study Association, believes that a father's position in the family has meaning not only for his wife, his children and himself, but for our whole society. Here are some of his ideas:

"To the young child . . . going to church may mean only doing something with father. But it may be on the basis of this sharing that he later develops his own religious interests. The same is true of children who have caught from their parents a real enjoyment of books, art and music. Often it is only the mother who shares in these pursuits. . . . A father's joining in such interests gives them greater richness and meaning for the future. . . ."

And the father, according to Dr. Dybwad, has an equally important job in interpreting to his child the community of which he is a part:

"He will let him learn about his job through visits to the office, through a Saturday excursion to the factory, through a ride on a milk truck . . . to give the child a positive feeling toward the job which deprives him so often of his father's company. . . . The child may not be able to understand the father's participation in community affairs. But he will get the feeling that Dad is doing something that will help not just him but others as well."

All of which means that Father must give not only time to his children, but he must give more of himself if he is to be a father in reality as well as in name. True, he must work; but work should not be used as an excuse to evade his responsibilities as a member of the human race. The kind of fathers who are always too busy to have time for Junior are the kind of men the late H. L. Mencken had in mind when he said: "Men work simply in order to escape the depressing agony of contemplating life . . . their work, like their play, is a mumbo-jumbo that serves them by permitting them to escape from reality."

Gordon H. Schroeder, in the *Christian Herald*, reports that three hundred seventh- and eighth-grade boys kept a record for two weeks of the amount of time each spent with his father. The average time father and son had alone together for an entire week was seven and one-half minutes!

This is the kind of dreary statistic that seems to bear out the contention of Philip Wylie, that acid critic of our social scene, that "the vast majority of American men are lousy fathers." * Mr. Wylie estimates that even the busiest man has approximately fifty-seven hours a week for eating, relaxing or doing as he pleases. Out of fifty-seven hours, surely he can spare more than seven and one-half minutes for his children. "But Dad has left home," concludes Mr. Wylie sadly. "He won't come back until it dawns on him that the most profound satisfactions in his life arise from being a father first, and only after that a top golfer or a big shot in business."

Fatherhood implies manhood. It is the visible seal of a man's physical maturity. Unfortunately for our children, it does not automatically confer maturity of the mind and spirit. A man must achieve that for himself.

Yes, it's time that Father came home. Just as it takes two people to produce a child. it also takes the moral influence of two people—mother and father—to create a happy, potentially useful individual.

---

* *Reader's Digest,* March, 1956.

3

HOW TO GET ALONG WITH MEN

OGDEN NASH, one of my favorite moderns, in his "Ode to the Father of Infant Female Children," bewails the fact that somewhere in the world is a baby boy who will grow up to be the man his lovely new baby daughter will eventually marry. While most fathers of charming girl babies feel the same way, let's face it: the only thing worse for a woman than a lifetime of catering to masculine whims is for her to have no male to cater to.

And since roughly half the population is male, getting along with men is every woman's problem. Husbands, fathers, sons and sons-in-law—bosses, customers, friends, suitors and wolves—doctors, lawyers, merchants, clerks—butchers, bakers and the Fuller Brush man. The list of men most of us have to come to terms with is delightfully endless.

Since it is pretty well established by this time that men and women differ somewhat from each other, it isn't a bad idea for women to give some thought to pleasing the male animal.

(If you are one of those women who resent the whole idea of bothering with the likes and dislikes of the brutes, don't waste your time here. You probably don't have any man trouble like the rest of us—or as much fun, either.)

What are the qualities men hopefully expect women to supply?

Number One on their list is comfort! And lest you think I got this answer from a group of superannuated playboys who were fed up with the champagne circuit, listen to this:

The question was asked in a survey of men in the armed forces at the end of World War II: "What do you expect to get out of married life?" And almost without exception, the hard-muscled lads in uniform sent the answer bouncing back. Not glamor, not excitement; just plain, old-fashioned comfort! This may be disappointing to many a palpitating miss who believes all she reads in the cosmetic and perfume ads; but, if comfort is what it takes, why not dish it out? Apparently an ounce of it is worth a pound of glamor. Only what, exactly, constitutes a man's idea of comfort? Someone who is easy on the eyes, the ears and the nerves? Whistler's Mother? Or Marilyn Monroe? Let's see.

Women in one of our courses discussed the subject of how they got along with men. From their experiences have evolved the following rules which seem to be effective:

1. *Be good-natured and understanding.*

Dorothy Dix once wrote that the first thing a man should look for in a wife was a good disposition. Any woman who wants to please any man, be her husband, boss, plumber or a three-month-old son, should be more concerned over her temper showing than her slip. A man would rather eat canned beans in an atmosphere of gaiety and charm than dine on filet mignon with a fretful, whining, nagging female.

A certain bachelor once confessed that if he had to make a choice of wife between a gay, good-natured, sunny-tempered, unfaithful woman and a virtuous shrew, he wouldn't hesitate—no Down-Beat Dolly for him!

My own husband, many years ago, employed a stenographer who, as a typist, was strictly for the birds. She couldn't spell, she was slow, she was inaccurate. But she kept her job until she got married and retired because she had the disposition of a rather jolly angel. She was proof against morning grouches, complaints and criticism. She lit up a room like sunshine. It was worth her salary just to have her around. I don't know whether her cooking is better than her shorthand, but I see her and her husband occasionally and it is quite

147

apparent that he doesn't care—his face lights up like a neon sign every time he looks at her.

2. *Be a good companion.*

Jack Fleck, U.S. Open Golf Champion, wrote a short article for the New York *World-Telegram*, in which he told how, against great odds, he managed to take over the golfing concessions of two municipal golf courses in Davenport, Iowa. It was a hard struggle, trying to maintain the concessions and at the same time work up his own golf game so that he could take a crack at the championship. It was only after marrying Lynn Burnsdale of Chicago that he found his opportunity. She threw herself into the business and ran the Pro shop while Jack put in more time on his golf game.

Finally, in 1952, Lynn, Jack and their thirteen-month old son Craig went on tour. Lynn remained in the background and cared for their son, while Jack played the tournaments. As he put it, "I never let Lynn follow me on the course. You don't see a postman's wife following hubby on the route."

Here was a wife who didn't actively participate in the game that to Jack Fleck was a hobby and a business. But she was there on the sidelines, interested and rooting for him. She was a good companion.

A student of one of my husband's classes told how she helped her husband's dream come true for him by learning to be a good companion.

Mrs. Florence Maynard who lives in a small town in northern New York state, was apparently an average wife. For the first sixteen years of their married life, she took care of her home-making, but something was lacking. Finally, she discovered what this lack was. It was companionship. Outside of their home, Mr. and Mrs. Maynard had few common interests. Mrs. Maynard took some steps to alter this situation.

"One of my husband's main interests was professional hockey," she said, "so my first step was to develop an interest in the game. Before I realized what was happening, I found myself getting tremendously excited by hockey too. I was as eager to go to the games as he was, and it was I who scanned the TV section of the paper for time schedules on televised games. Not only did I enjoy my own interest in this exciting sport, but I found I was doing things too, instead of sitting home alone while my husband had all the fun.

"From hockey, I went on to learn more about his other interests and am now sharing fun with the man I married and for whom I just kept a home for sixteen years."

3. *Be a good listener.*

Nearly all men subscribe to the popular myth that women talk too much. What they mean is that they don't get a chance themselves to talk too much.

What many women who wish to please men in this respect fail to understand is that listening isn't just sitting silent like Patience on a monument while a man yammers happily on. It is the *quality* of listening that inspires, and listening is an *active* quality. You can even get a word in edgewise yourself, if you become a really accomplished listener.

Listening means, first, giving attention. No roving eyes, or nervous, fidgety movements. Don't let your mind wander to tomorrow's grocery list or the new dress you would like to buy. If you concentrate, who knows? You might learn something. And while you listen, relax your features and let them follow through. Nothing puts off a speaker like a dead-pan audience. One of a stage director's hard jobs is to train actors to appear to be listening to what another actor in a play is saying. If you want to please a man, train yourself the same way.

Good listening involves both concentration and co-operation. There used to be a theory that all a girl had to do to reduce a guy to the melting point was look up at him while he described his big deal with Continental Can and murmur the equivalent of "You great big wonderful dream-boat. My, what a genius!" The dumber she was, the harder he fell. Well, the script has changed a little. Aside from the fact that so many girls are successfully handling their own big deals these days and find the switch from head buyer to admiring bird-brain a little abrupt, men seem to be getting smart enough to tell the difference between a gal who really cares what he's talking about and a clinging vine who is shopping for a sturdy oak to drape herself around. So, if you want to win or influence a man, don't offer him the synthetic, sugar-coated wide-eyed routine, when all he wants is an intelligent listener.

Ask a question now and then, a good one that shows

you hear what he's saying and want to hear more. Bring up an occasional difference of opinion as a stimulant. If you have any experience of your own that backs up what he's saying, throw it in while he catches his breath; but make it brief. Return him the conversational ball.

This kind of listening is not mere sufferance of a monologue, but a two-way experience in communication.

Most people are poor listeners because they haven't worked at it long enough to be familiar with the rules. We can all improve ourselves by practice. Skillful listeners almost always turn out to be good talkers themselves, too, when they go to bat—one skill promotes the other.

The art of good listening, once acquired, will not only help us to get along better with men, but with other kinds of people, too. It will also help us to mature, because it is one of the ways by which we learn.

4. *Be adaptable.*

"Let's ask Jim and Mabel over tonight," says the man of the house. "Haven't seen old Jim in a dog's age." "All right," says his nearest and dearest, "but I'd better call Helen and Tom too, because they've had us twice lately. And then—oh, dear!—Helen's sister is visiting them, and I'll have to get an extra man for her. You'll have to run down to the delicatessen and get more beer and some of those crunchy cheese crackers. I'll get on the phone and then I'll have to fix my face and change my dress and pick things up a little. You can run the vacuum while I change." By this time, her husband is wishing he had kept his big mouth shut. All he wanted in the first place was a quiet, neighborly get-together with a couple of friends, but he finds himself caught up in the flurry of a full-scale evening's entertainment.

For some reason, women find it difficult to do anything on spur-of-the-moment impulse, unless it is to buy a hat. No man understands this. He can't figu why women insist on planning an evening at the theater weeks in advance, or why, when he suggests an impromptu week end in the country, the little woman says she hasn't a thing to wear and let's wait until next week so she can notify the milkman.

Granted that masculine impulses are often trying to the orderly female mind, what's to lose by saying, "Yes, let's," once in a while instead of, "Yes, but . . ." One of the happiest wives I know has a husband who likes short vacations and who is prone to phone at the drop of a travel folder and say, "Pack up, honey—we're off to Bermuda tomorrow morning." His wife, who is an old China hand at this sort of thing, throws her bathing suit into a suitcase, farms out the parakeet with neighbors, cancels appointments and is actually ready to board that boat the next morning. She says it's nothing, really, any wife can do the same with a little practice.

When I was young, it was considered the kiss of death to a girl's popularity if she accepted a date at the last minute—it was tantamount to a confession that she was available only because nobody else had asked her. Well, perhaps being this hard to get gains a girl a fine reputation, but it loses her an awful lot of fun. So what if he did ask for a date with somebody else first? It gives us a chance to prove that second choices are often best. Being adaptable to a man's moods is one of the surest ways to win his heart.

When a man gets an idea, he likes to translate it into action now, at once, immediately! The balkiness of women in falling in with these masculine impulses is a constant irritant to the sterner sex. The gal who learns early in life to adapt to a man's moods has come a long way toward penetrating the mystery of getting along with men.

5. *Be efficient, but not officious.*

A girl in one of our classes once told about losing a highly eligible beau because she was too competent. This girl had a good job and spent her days running an office, planning, giving orders and taking responsibility. She couldn't throw her gears into reverse on social occasions. "I found myself," she confessed, "hailing taxis successfully while my date was still opening the umbrella; punching elevator buttons for him; recommending that he order liver and bacon at dinner to help his blood count; he never had a chance to hold a chair for me or help me off with my coat or put on my overshoes because, busy little bee that I am, I always did it first. I wasn't just efficient—I was officious, a helpful Henrietta who helped myself right out of his life."

Pity today's poor working girl, because, all too often,

when the right man enters her life she's too busy being successful and independent and capable to remember she's also a woman. Man, spoiled creature, not only wants to eat his cake and have it—he wants it to have the nourishing qualities of home-baked bread. He wants a girl with the feminine appeal of Elaine the Lily Maid and brains enough to appreciate him—and, if necessary, help him add to the family income.

To make him feel like this is what he is getting when he picks you isn't so hard as it sounds. Be as efficient as all get-out on the job, an eager beaver for the boss, but after office hours allow your man the luxury of feeling he's dating a woman, not a brain.

I learned this, as most women do, from one of the ones that got away. Years ago, I enjoyed the friendship of a personable young man who escorted me frequently, that is, for a while. About that time, I got interested in local politics and spent a lot of my leisure in this exciting activity. When I wasn't campaigning or going to meetings, I was talking to my date about what Judge So-and-So said and explaining to him what was wrong with the administration. Finally he spelled it out for me. "You used to be a girl," he said. "Now you're a walking campaign leaflet. If I want a lecture on political philosophy, I'll write a letter to my congressman. In the meantime, I'm available for some good woman who wants to brighten up my evenings."

When last heard from, he was happily married to a curvaceous blonde who runs his home efficiently and well, but who never forgets she's a girl.

6. *Be yourself.*

Nothing is more comic to a man than to see a sixty-plus female squeezed into Junior Miss clothes, sporting drugstore-dyed hair, tottering along in three-inch heels and topped off by falsies that fool nobody. Of all the pathetic spectacles, the woman who digs in her heels and refuses to accept maturity is perhaps the most pitiable. She is convinced that feminine charm is a matter of age and that if she tries hard enough no one will ever take her for a day over thirty-nine. It takes a strong stomach to watch a woman of this type ogling and simpering at a man in a desperate effort to ensnare him with her imaginary sex appeal.

Nor is this the only way in which women sin against the cardinal rule of maturity—be yourself. A quiet, modest girl sometimes imagines that she will increase her attractiveness by loud laughter, too many drinks and other antics which she imagines will transform her into the life and soul of the party. Contrary to what some women believe, men are not so stupid at sizing us up for what we really are. They know a hawk from a handsaw.

The immature notion that one can get and hold a man by "changing the personality," altering make-up, getting a new dress and hairdo, and thus hypnotize him so that he won't know what he's getting is widely held by a number of otherwise intelligent women. No one can change her personality, and what's wrong with using the one God gave us? All we need do is take the wraps off and let it shine. We can develop our good

155

qualities and eliminate our less attractive ones. We can be our best selves. And that's all anyone should expect of anyone else, whatever the sex.

7. *Be glad you're a woman.*

Whoever coined that disgusting phrase, "battle of the sexes," must have had a king-sized chip on his shoulder. Why men and women should fight each other simply because they are men and women has never been clear to me. There are so many other issues worth fighting about.

At any rate, the woman who regards all men as enemies, who believes that women are put upon by nature and mankind, who is convinced that every man is out to take advantage of every woman is scarcely going to endear herself to the male sex. She doesn't care, because she hates men anyway—she says.

To achieve any important relationship with any man, a woman must first of all be glad to be a woman. She must accept the biological fact that woman has a specific role in human affairs, and respect that fundamental female function. Rejection of one's femininity is not confined to what the world calls "old maids." In my experience, the middle-aged unmarried women I have known have been, on the whole, exceptionally mature, healthy-minded and charming. And I have known married women who bitterly complained that "being a woman was to be a second-class citizen," that "nature certainly played favorites when she created the two sexes," and all the rest of the battle-of-the-sexes guff.

The joyful acceptance of one's sex is not dependent upon marital status; it is the result of healthy attitudes and emotional maturity. Without this basic acceptance, happiness between men and women cannot be attained, and one of life's most important areas of fulfillment is reduced to a battleground.

Getting along with men cannot be reduced to a precise formula, bound up as it is in the depths and shallows, lights and shadows of individual personality. But the few rules sketched in this chapter at least point the way for greater understanding of the opposite sex. In the better world we all long for, men and women will not be ranged against each other like natural enemies, but will work, love and play together with hands and hearts joined in friendship and love.

4

THE REDISCOVERY OF LOVE

LOVE IS ONE OF THE most talked-about subjects in the world, and the least understood. It has inspired artists since the beginning of time, it is the foundation of marriage and the family—and loss or lack of it can shatter a human personality or prevent its normal development.

Most of us have a narrow-gauge, one-track conception of love. We think of it exclusively in terms of family or sex relationships. More often than not, we confuse and adulterate it with possessiveness, self-esteem, appeasement and dependence.

Until fairly recently, love has not been considered a subject for serious scientific attention. Today, things are different. A number of researchers, psychologists, doctors and scientists have been giving more study and thought to love as a basic need of human beings and a vast, unexplored source of influence and power in the affairs of mankind. In the light of these findings, we may have to overhaul and extend some of our preconceived notions about love.

What does love have to do with maturity? Dr. Rollo May answers that question. In his recent book: *Man's Search for Himself,* he writes: "To be capable of giving and receiving mature love is as sound a criterion as we have for the fulfilled personality."

Dr. May also asserts that most people do not know how to give or receive love, and that the average person's conception of love is both sentimental and infantile.

The woman, for example, who devotes her life so exclusively to catering to husband and children that she literally shuts out the rest of the world is not so much loving as possessive. Real love doesn't confine itself, it extends itself. The man who worships his mother to the extent that he can never find a wife to compare with her should not be admired as a model of a "loving" son—he is a case of arrested emotional development and still in an infantile state of dependence. Clinging is not the same as loving.

Perhaps it is easier to define the kind of love that strengthens and matures a personality by first finding out what it *isn't*.

First of all, it bears little relation to the boy-meets-girl, orchids-and-champagne type of romance we so often see in the movies, or the grand passion of sex exploitation dear to the hearts of novelists. Love is not confined to the young and the beautiful.

Dr. Abraham Stone, urological specialist and President of the American Association of Marriage Counselors, tells us that many times when we say, "I love," we really mean, "I desire," "I want to possess," "I get gratification from," "I exploit," or even, "I feel guilty about." This is what scientists call "pseudo-love."

Many parents use "love" as an excuse for overindulgence of their children. Actually, they are buying off their children instead of helping them grow and develop. Children's Village, at Dobbs Ferry, New York, is a project devoted to retraining troubled youngsters who need guidance. Director Harold P. Strong says, "Every day we are undoing the damage done by parents who have confused the word 'love' with 'appeasement.'"

The mature concept of love is the kind Jesus was talking about when he said: "Thou shalt love thy neighbor as thyself." It is the kind of love Plato analyzed in the *Symposium,* which begins with a personal relationship and broadens until it includes all humanity and the universe itself. The elements of love are always the same whether it is love between husband and wife, parent and child or man and humanity.

True love between individuals does not stifle growth; it affirms another personality and encourages it to grow and develop.

I have known parents, and so have you, who resented a daughter's marriage solely because it would mean that the daughter would have to set up her new home in some distant place. I remember hearing one woman wail, "Why couldn't Joan have married one of our home-town boys? Then we could see her often. All our lives, we have struggled to give her advantages, and she repays us by marrying somebody who will force

160

her to live half a continent away from her own family!"

This woman would have been shocked to be told that she did not love her daughter. But she was confusing possessiveness and self-gratification with love.

Real love does not clutch the loved one in a tight fist; it opens its hand and lets go. The mature personality does not desire to keep anyone in emotional slavery. It wants freedom for the loved one, as well as for itself. Like any other creative force, love lives and has its being in freedom.

I like the definition of love given by writer Priscilla Robertson in *Harper's* magazine. Love, says Mrs. Robertson, "means giving someone what he needs, for his own sake, not yours. It is also the way you feel when you are given something you need. Love includes the feelings of a parent who gives a child independence as he needs it, but not the sort of exploitation that leads to 'momism.' It includes various kinds of sexual relationships, but not the use of sex in the frantic pursuit of self-esteem or youth. My definition includes the response you give to those few persons—teachers and friends—who manage somehow to show you who you are and what you may become. And it includes charity, encompassing the whole person, neither the giving of a stone when a man asks for bread, nor the giving of bread when he asks for understanding.

"We all know 'well-meaning' people who continually bungle their favors," continues Mrs. Robertson. "They press on us things we don't want and withhold through apparent obtuseness what we do want. I would not include these people among the loving ones, and I think psychologists agree that at the back of their seeming stupidity lies a concealed hostility."

Nothing is more misleading than the old saying: "Love is blind." Only with the eyes of love can we see the truth about our fellow man. All of us have a self that is unseen by the casual or the indifferent, a sensitive, inarticulate self that we often bury from the sight of others for fear it will be hurt or misunderstood. We assume various poses or disguises to hide it—silence, shyness, aggressiveness, toughness. But we always cherish a secret hope that someone will care enough for us to discover what we really are inside. Love alone has this special insight into the human heart. It is the answer to that eternal question: "What does she see in him?"

To delight in the growth and development of our loved ones, to affirm and encourage their unique individuality, to respect their integrity and provide an emotional atmosphere of freedom and affection, these are the attitudes we must have if we would learn to love. Love provides the soil, atmosphere and nourishment in which others may grow.

Jealousy is an emotion often confused with love. Actually, it is a result of lack of confidence in our own powers to inspire affection, as well as a desire to possess and enslave another. It can be conquered by replacing this desire to possess with the desire to give.

Here is a true story of a woman who successfully overcame jealousy and learned to love. She says:

"Ten years ago, I was caught in the iron grip of jealousy. I lived in constant fear of losing my husband.

Not that he gave me any cause for jealousy. I would have suffered less if he had, because then I would have been spared the humiliating knowledge that my fears were neurotic and imaginary. I was obsessed to the point where I behaved like wives in cartoon comics, feverishly searching my husband's pockets and examining the contents of the ash tray in the car. I often cried myself to sleep and spent my day building up new suspicions.

"One day I looked in my mirror. I saw an unlovely sight—myself. Stringy hair, no make-up, a haggard, strained look—and my clothes looked like a sack draped on a broomstick! 'So, Helen,' I said to myself, 'you're afraid of losing your man. Could you blame him if you did? What are you going to do about it?' I decided on a plan of campaign. I began to spend less time on waxing the floors and polishing the furniture and more on making myself attractive. I rested every afternoon and put on some much-needed weight. I got a job selling cosmetics and learned to apply them on myself to advantage. And as I began to look better and feel better, I found that my attitude was changing. My husband felt this change in me and responded in a way that banished the clouds of self-doubt and suspicion forever from my mind. I harnessed the energy I had been wasting on jealousy and set it in channels that made me the kind of wife I knew my husband wanted me to be."

This woman acquired the ability to love once she realized that love does not dictate—it affirms.

When we find these foreign elements of possession,

jealousy and domination creeping into our souls, the genuine love we have for others is gradually dimmed out. The most beautiful garden in the world will, in time, become a wilderness if the weeds are allowed to grow unchecked.

One of the tragedies of family relationship is that so often we do not realize what harm we are doing to others in the name of love. The overstrict parent tells himself "it is for the child's own good" that he stifles and confines. The overindulgent say that they are motivated by desire for the "happiness" of their children.

Mrs. S. F. Allen, of Columbus, Ohio, tells a moving story of her dilemma in this respect. Some years ago, Mrs. Allen found herself, after a divorce from her husband, with the responsibility of caring for herself and two children, and she was overwhelmed by the responsibility of being both father and mother to them. She felt it was her duty to be strict in order to raise them properly.

"I laid down the law," said Mrs. Allen. "And no excuses were accepted. I didn't talk things over with the children or bother to hear their side of a story—I told them exactly what to do and when to do it. They had no chance for independent thinking, only a set of rules to be obeyed.

"A subtle change pervaded our home. The children began to shy away from me. They evaded any attempts on my part to be affectionate. Finally I realized that they were afraid of me, of their own mother!

"I did some pretty honest thinking and came to the conclusion that, subconsciously, I had not been acting

164

for the children's good at all—I had been taking out on them my own repressed resentments over the divorce. I was making them suffer for my mistakes. No wonder that they felt this, and, without being able to understand it, reacted accordingly.

"I set about breaking up this pattern I had unknowingly forced upon them. I prayed God for guidance and began to see my children in a new light, as individuals, rather than as burdens or responsibilities. They were people as I was, and I set about treating them that way. Instead of hurrying home from work to a full schedule of household duties, I began to let some of the housework go in order to enjoy my children, play games with them or take them to interesting places. I learned to guide them instead of merely commanding them.

"As my heart relaxed and opened up, laughter and song crept back into our home. Love, affection and happiness reflected from me to the children, and renewed and strengthened our relationships with each other. All our problems became easier to meet and solve in this atmosphere."

Mrs. Allen learned to love, and the therapy of love healed the wounds in her home life.

Our ability to love not only affects our intimate family relationships, but determines our ability to get along with other people as well. Our attitudes to our friends, our jobs, our community and the world are largely determined by the kind of love we have given and received within our family.

Psychologist Milton Greenblatt says: "If a child is

loved and accepted, he learns to be happy with himself, to love members of his family, and finally to regard all men with genuine altruistic concern."

Dr. Ashley Montagu, in his book *The Direction of Human Development,* tells us that to live and to love are properly the same thing, as almost every religion has insisted. He concludes: "It seems now clear that the main principle by which human beings must guide the future course of their development is love."

The idea that love must be properly confined only to family members and close friends is mistaken; the more we love, the more we can love. Love is vital energy which informs and charges the whole personality and spills its radiance over all of our activities. The loving person is filled with enthusiasm for his work, his fellow creatures, for life itself. He is apt to live longer and stay healthier.

Certainly, it is immensely important to ourselves and others to acquire this mature concept of love. In this nation alone, over 400,000 marriages are wrecked by divorce each year, and many thousands of others resemble battlegrounds. Nations, races and groups all over the world are divided and hostile. Man's most important problem is to learn to live in harmony with his fellow man if he is to survive.

It is heartening to realize that science is beginning to explore the immense possibilities of "love-energy," to devote its resources to this area of knowledge. An outstanding example is the Harvard Research Center in Creative Altruism, directed by Sociologist Pitirim A. Sorokin.

All of which goes to show that perhaps we are beginning to catch up with Jesus. Two thousand years ago, he was laying down the principles of mental, moral and spiritual health when he said:

"Love thine enemies. . . ." "God is love." "A new commandment I give unto you, That ye love one another."

PART IV IN A CAPSULE

MARRIAGE IS FOR GROWNUPS

How to Get Along With Women. Here are seven ways:

1. Give her appreciation.
2. Be generous and considerate.
3. Keep yourself attractive.
4. Understand a woman's work.
5. Be dependable.
6. Share her interests.
7. Love her.

Father Come Home. Children need fathers too.

How to Get Along With Men. Here are seven ways:

1. Be good-natured.
2. Be a good companion.
3. Be a good listener.
4. Be adaptable.
5. Be efficient, not officious.
6. Be yourself.
7. Be glad you're a woman.

The Rediscovery of Love. We must develop a more mature concept of love.

PART **five**

MATURITY

AND MAKING FRIENDS

1

LONELINESS: THE GREAT AMERICAN DISEASE

FIVE YEARS AGO death took the husband of a friend of mine. Since that time, she, like thousands of others, has been suffering from that dread disease called loneliness.

"What will I do?" she implored me one evening, a month after her husband's death. "Where will I live? How can I ever be happy again?"

I tried to explain that, since her anxiety stemmed from the personal tragedy that took her husband from her while they were still in their fifties, she would shed this cloak of grief and worry when the wheels stopped spinning. I told her she would build a new life, a new form of happiness, from the ashes of the old.

"No," she replied drearily, "I don't believe I will ever be really happy again. I'm not a young woman any more. My children are all grown up and married, and there'll be no place for me."

The poor woman had been stricken with a double-strength case of pernicious self-pity combined with a complete lack of understanding of the care and treatment of the disease.

The years passed, during which time I observed the progress of the patient. There wasn't any progress.

"Surely," I said to her once, "you don't think you're someone set apart for sympathy and pity. You can rebuild your life, cultivate new friends and new interests to substitute for those of the past."

She listened but she didn't hear. She was feeling too sorry for herself. Finally she decided she would make her children responsible for her happiness and she moved in with a married daughter.

It was a harrowing experience for everyone and was climaxed by a degrading scene of name-calling and insult that turned the daughter against her mother. She moved to her son's home, but it was not much better.

Finally, she was provided with her own apartment, but this wasn't the answer either. Her own family didn't want her any more, she told me in tears one afternoon.

This woman will always be unhappy as long as she expects the world to be sorry for her. She's a bitter, selfish woman and, although today she's sixty-one years of age, she's still a child emotionally.

Many lonely people never understand that love and friendship don't come gift-wrapped in some shiny package. Popularity and acceptance are never achieved by an invitation brought in on a silver platter.

People have to make an effort to be liked. They cannot take love and friendship and good times as something due them under the terms of a contract.

Let's face up to the stark truth. Husbands die, wives die, but there's no statute of limitations on their survivors' right to happiness. What they must understand, however, is that it must be worked for, not taken for granted as a dole or a handout. They have to *make* themselves liked and wanted.

Picture for a moment a cruise ship skimming the blue waters of the Mediterranean. Many happily married couples are aboard for vacation trips, along with scores of unattached young people. And moving among the joyful band of tourists is a bright, smiling woman in her sixties, traveling alone.

This is how she grabbed the brass ring of happiness on the second ride around. She, too, lost her husband, grieved just as much as my other friend, but she awoke one morning, cast aside the robes of mourning and embarked upon a new life. It was a decision reached through deep thought and planning.

Her husband had been her love and her life, but now this was over. She had always had a second interest, her painting, her water colors, and she busily set about pursuing this art. What once was a hobby now became a vitally important activity. Not only did it keep her occupied during those long days of sorrow, but it eventually led to a remunerative business that gave her the greatest reward—independence.

For a time, she found it difficult to meet people, to assert herself, because for so long her husband had been her constant companion and her strength. She was not beautiful, she was not wealthy, and in those days of doubt and despair she asked herself what she could do, how she could act so that people would accept her and desire her company.

Then the answer came. She would have to *make* herself wanted; she would have to give of herself, rather than expect that others would give of themselves.

She dried the tears and replaced them with a smile. She kept busy with her painting. She called on old friends, and made a point of being gay. She laughed and she joked—and never stayed too long. And then, before she quite realized it, she was being sought after as a dinner guest. And she was asked to display her paintings at the Community House.

The days and the months passed, and there came the night when she was on this cruise ship on the Mediterranean. She was the most sought-after passenger on the ship. She was friendly with everyone, but stayed aloof from any entanglement. She never let herself be a hanger-on.

The night before the ship docked, the gayest party aboard was in her stateroom. In her unassuming way she was repaying the invitations that had been showered upon her during the trip.

This woman has made many such trips since that time. She has learned that she must wade out into the mainstream of life and contribute, if she is to be wanted. Wherever she walks, she creates an atmosphere of friendliness. She's nice to be near.

In spite of the great strides made by modern medicine and miracle drugs, our century has developed a new ailment—the loneliness of the crowd.

Lynn White, Jr., president of Mills College in Oakland, California, once delivered a noteworthy address on this type of loneliness to an audience attending a YWCA dinner.

"The great disease of the twentieth century is loneliness," he declared. "To use David Riesman's term, we are 'the lonely crowd.' As the population has grown and as it has agglomerated into vast oceans of humanity, the sense of an intelligible community has largely been lost. . . . The vast impersonality of the world in which we live, the scale of our business and government, the frequency with which people move from one place to another—failing, as a rule, in each place to form lasting friendships: all of these are merely aspects of the new ice age which is chilling the hearts of untold millions."

And Dr. White summarizes well when he says that "the love of God and of one's fellow man is a single passion. Only so will we be able to combat the personal and cosmic loneliness which corrodes the soul. Only so will we foster a climate of courage."

Those who would conquer loneliness must indeed live in Dr. White's "climate of courage." We must develop warm relationships wherever we go and rely on our own Bunsen burner to create the warmth and the friendliness.

If we would conquer loneliness, we must leave the shadows of self-pity and walk into the bright light of adventure in meeting new people and making new friends. We must walk gaily into places where we can share what we have to offer with those equally eager to share with us.

Naturally, it takes courage, but most people undersell themselves. The governors they place on their accelerators never let them out of low gear on the express-ways of life.

Statistics seem to indicate that most married women outlive their husbands and, admittedly, it is more difficult for a woman to carve out a new life once her husband is gone. Man's work, by the very nature of its requirements, forces him to make more of an effort to push himself forward. He is the stronger, more aggressive member of the partnership. The woman, in most cases, fulfills her part of the agreement with her interests centered on the home and the family. She is not so readily prepared to go it alone and find happiness along the way. But she can do it, if she decides to grow up and not just grow old.

But loneliness is not confined to the widow or the widower. It can haunt the bachelor and the beauty queen, strike the stranger in the city and the soloist in the country church.

A few years ago, a young eligible bachelor came to New York, planning to paint the town a bright shade of crimson. He was tall and handsome; he was well educated and well traveled; he had charm and he knew it. He reached the big city, he attended his sales meetings during the day, and then found he was lonely in the evenings. He hated eating alone, and he despised sitting alone in a movie house. He shied away from imposing on the married friends he had in the city. And, let's say it, he didn't want a girl thrown at him.

Naturally, he wanted to meet nice girls, but he didn't want to pick one up at a Greenwich Village bar or to enroll in a lonely hearts' club or one of the social introduction services that try to solve this particular problem. The result was that he spent a miserable time in a city where he had expected to have a big fling.

I know a city can be lonelier than any country town. I also know that a man has to put forth just that much extra effort in a city to place himself where he will be accepted and wanted. He must determine, in advance, where his after-hours interests lie and then explore those places. He must want people with similar interests to accept him, but he usually must light the fire himself.

A man moving into a new city can do many things. He will engender friendships by joining a church and a club that suits some special interest. He may find friendship and companionship in adult education courses. The point is that he will never achieve the acceptance he so earnestly desires by eating alone at the Brass Rail or sitting alone at the Roxy. He has to do something for himself. New York's subway is just about the greatest underground transportation in the world, but it's utterly useless to you unless you are willing to drop in a token and walk through the turnstile.

Several years ago, I became acquainted with two girls who shared an apartment on New York City's east side. Both were attractive, both held well-paying jobs and both, naturally, wanted to be popular. One of these girls, with surprising wisdom for her youth, recognized that life, especially for a single girl in a big city, must be carefully planned. She joined a church and actively participated in its programs and projects. She enrolled in a discussion club, even took a personality-improvement course. She worked at meeting nice people and creating a full life on a working girl's salary.

She entertained modestly but joyously. She carefully planned her social relationships and avoided the dubious distinction of being paired up with every Tom, Dick, etc.

Certainly, she was lonely when she came to New York. What girl isn't—in New York or Topeka or Bash Bish Falls? But, like the man who dived a hundred feet into a wet sponge, she told herself she didn't like it, and she did something about it.

Today she is an even closer friend of mine; I see her often. She is happily married to a brilliant young lawyer. She has achieved a wonderful life, and the accent is on the achievement.

Her roommate? She was lonely too, but she went thataway. She sought out friends, but, unfortunately, they were all sitting on bar stools. Finally, she joined a club too.

It was Alcoholics Anonymous!

2
_____

PEOPLE ARE WONDERFUL

"ONE MORNING about eleven o'clock, without any warning whatsoever, I lost my company."

That's the way the letter started out, a letter from Joni Lea Lowrie, of 36 East Thirty-sixth Street, New York City. She wanted to tell me about people, wonderful people.

"The company was taken from me by two businessmen through a legal technicality," she continued. "I was stunned. I checked with my attorney and found there was nothing I could do. Believe me, I have never in my life been so worried and afraid. Everything I owned was gone. About two o'clock I went out to the factory and told Louise, my production manager, what had happened. I then said good-by to each of the other workers. Most of them had been with me since I had started the company.

"At quitting time an incredible thing happened. Every person in the factory and the office packed up his personal belongings and quit. The new owners offered them everything if they would return. They offered Louise a lifetime job if she would come back and she said, 'I don't have to work for people like you.' The owners were frantic. They had a lot of inventory and machines, but they didn't know how to produce a single number and not one employee would work for them.

"The workers applied for unemployment benefits, but when the company was called, the owners said, 'We have jobs for these people. Send them back to work.' The workers refused, so, of course, they couldn't get compensation. I had nothing to offer them; I had nothing myself. Everything was tied up in my business.

"This went on for five weeks. I honestly don't know how the workers lived, because most of them spent every penny of income immediately. But, at the end of that time, the new owners conceded defeat. They had an empty shell, really, because they couldn't produce. The company was legally returned to me one afternoon about four o'clock and the next morning every employee was back on the job.

"When I lost my company the worst that could possibly happen did happen. There was absolutely nothing I could do about it. The only thing in my favor was that such sincere respect, appreciation and understanding had always existed between my employees and me that when trouble came they reacted with great loyalty, so much so that they literally forced the return of the company to me. I am humble and grateful for what they did. No one in the world could have more wonderful friends than the people in my organization."

It's quite a story! But people—mature people, that is—are discovering every day the wonders of what we call mankind. It's the inexperienced, immature person who says that all politicians are crooks, that big business is merciless, that "the boss" is a knucklehead.

Dal Perry, from West Point, Virginia, had occasion to learn a lesson in point when he was at sea on a liberty ship in 1944. Mr. Perry had the rank of Deck Cadet Midshipman, the lowest on board. He had to take orders from everyone and talk back to no one. A bad report from any officer and, whoosh, he would have been in the army.

As Mr. Perry tells it: "The Captain despised the Cadet system and resented everything and everybody connected with the Merchant Marine Academy. Consequently, he made life a living hell for me. That old captain drove me far more than Captain Bligh ever thought of driving his men on the *Bounty*.

"After four weeks of this unmerciful treatment, I realized that something had to give. I was behind in my studies, on which I was to spend six hours a day. I finally decided I would have to sell myself to that skipper and that night I got one of my books and sheepishly knocked on his door.

" 'Who's that?' barked his stern voice.

" 'It's Perry, Captain, I——'

" 'What the hell do you want?' he growled.

" 'I would appreciate very much, sir, if you would help me with a question I cannot answer. I know, in

181

your experience at sea, you have been in this situation a number of times and knew just what to do.'

" 'Very well,' the captain snapped. 'Let's see it.'

"When I left his quarters he had set aside four hours a day for me to study undisturbed; two hours of work on deck and one four-hour watch to stand. The captain turned out to be an understanding, wonderful man."

Everywhere we look, if a scowl doesn't fog up our vision, we will see mountains of evidence of the goodness, the kindness, the generosity of that wonderful fellow we call our fellow man.

How could anyone have survived the ravaging flood waters of the Mad River in Connecticut in the summer of 1955 and not have been inspired by the courage and the charity of his neighbors? Every time death and disaster strike this land of ours, we learn a new and wonderful lesson on the resources of people.

A friend of mine recently engaged in a bitter small-town political fight that estranged him from everyone in his particular neighborhood. A few months later he was terribly injured in an accident and taken to a New York City hospital.

On Christmas Eve, the saddest of all nights in a hospital, he looked up from his hospital bed to see two of his neighbors, whom he thought had hated him, standing at his side. In their arms they carried a tremendous Christmas stocking, a five-foot-long blue stocking filled to overflowing with gaily wrapped presents.

I would labor the point if I made any comment on what this incident did to my friend's feeling about people.

I'll always believe that most people are wonderful, in my town and in yours. And if I ever discover myself doubting it, I reach into a little drawer in my library at home and reread a letter I have kept there for a long time.

It was written by a Mrs. May Carley and these are her words:

"When I was twelve years of age, my father, who was a farmer, loaned a neighbor $1800 to keep him from losing his farm. A few years passed and the debt was not paid, although the neighbor was not pressed for money.

"The neighbor, who drank quite a lot, conceived the idea that, if he killed my father, he would not have to pay the debt. So, one night as father was driving into town, the neighbor deliberately cut across the road and ran into my father's car, breaking three of my father's ribs and badly hurting one hand and arm. The neighbor, who was unhurt, then drove away, leaving my father out on the road, hurt and alone.

"Some one in town heard of the incident and went out and got my father, brought him into town and went for a doctor. While my father was sitting on a curb of the sidewalk holding his ribs with one hand as he waited for the doctor, the drunken neighbor walked up to him and kicked him under the jaw with the toe of his boot. It not only cut a gash in my father's jaw but burst certain glands, subsequently poisoning other glands in his body.

"The doctor arrived shortly, along with the police. But my father refused to swear out a warrant against his neighbor, saying he was drunk and didn't know what he was doing. Having the man arrested, he said, would only cause more trouble for the man's family.

"My father was taken to a hospital in town where he spent almost a year and a half before he finally passed away. But, before he died, he called his five children to his bedside and talked to each of us separately.

"With me, he took my hand in his and said, 'Promise me you will never mistreat or say an unkind word to any of our neighbor's children so that they, like you, will grow up to be respected citizens in this community where we have always lived. You can't be happy with hatred in your heart.'

"That was the hardest promise to keep that ever came from a child's heart. But I am glad to say after thirty years that I have kept the promise and the neighbor's children are among my very best friends today."

What a depth of compassion and understanding this godly man must have possessed. His neighbor had taken his money and his life; yet, he bore him no ill will and he made certain that his family would bear him none after he was gone.

Dr. Willard Crosley, of 1535 Ben Lomand Drive, Glendale, California, has told me a rather amusing but enlightening experience of his student days when he was in his third year of medical school. It seems that, on the Saturday morning when the school dean was to give an important lecture on pharmacology, young Crosley decided to cut class and go on a picnic with a pretty blond nurse. Just when he was starting to recite a poem, he heard the clump, clump of approaching feet.

"I looked up," writes Dr. Crosley, "and stared into the face of the dean who, with his daughter, was taking a hike to gather herbs. I didn't get up, I didn't say anything, I froze with fear. He looked at me, scowled and walked away. When he left, panic set in. No longer was I interested in the picnic nor in my blond friend. All I could think about was that after three years of medical school I would be flunked out.

"I went back to the fraternity house and told my brothers about the episode. They all agreed it was a serious situation. One of them patted me on the back and said, 'Well, maybe you weren't meant to be a doctor.' Others asked me how much they could buy my books for. I spent a miserable week end.

"Monday morning I resolved to talk to the dean, and when I found him I said, 'Dean, I want to apologize for being so discourteous last Saturday. I didn't stand up, I didn't greet you and I acted without thinking.' The dean seemed amused and said:

"'Willard, in my youthful experiences I have had similar episodes. Think nothing of it. The important thing is, did you have a good time?'

"This completely relaxed me. I understood the dean was human; he had not forgotten how youth lives, works and plays. Perhaps that's why he was dean!"

Yes, Dr. Crosley, that's why he was the dean. That's why wonderful people all over the world have found happiness and success by cultivating mature attitudes.

It's the difference between daylight and darkness on the road of life.

J. W. Abbott, Jr., of 225 Hillside Avenue, Cranford, New Jersey, has been frank in describing how he gained a new appreciation of people when he was recalled into the navy to act as chief engineer on a destroyer being put into commission in San Diego.

"True to the navy tradition, they had picked me, a dumb accountant, to put in charge of all the firerooms, engine rooms and all the other machinery and equipment on the ship," says Mr. Abbott.

"Talk about fear and worry! I hadn't been in an engine room a half-dozen times in my life. I not only made myself sick worrying about it for the month while I was waiting to leave but it was even worse for the first few weeks I was on the ship. Actually, there was no need for this worry, because things were beginning to shape up and we were getting the machinery in working order.

"After we had worked on the ship for about a month, we were all given a three-day week-end pass. I called our men to quarters to pass out the good news. And just because it seemed the thing to do, I told them we were getting this extra leave because of the fine work they had been doing this past month. I told them how much I appreciated the cooperation they had been giving me, how well each man had accepted responsibility and that all this added together had made up an engineering department that was hard to beat.

"At the time I made those remarks, I didn't appreciate their real significance. A few days later though, it hit me like a ton of bricks. Here was the absolute truth! These men *were* accepting their responsibilities; they were doing a fine job; they were doing the very jobs that I was worrying about getting done.

"Here I had thought that I was shouldering the full load! Right then and there I came to my senses. I stopped being afraid we were going to blow the ship apart or worrying that we wouldn't be ready in time for commissioning. The lesson I learned from this is that we are not in this thing alone. There are always a lot of wonderful people around to lend us support when we need it, just as we lend our support to others."

Yes, the world is full of wonderful people. True, humanity also has its share of crooks and creeps, bums, swindlers, jerks and assorted villains. It's almost impossible to get through life without encountering a certain percentage of them. It takes a measure of maturity to realize that, just as one swallow doesn't make a summer, the occasional bad apple does not contaminate the whole human race.

It often happens that our own attitudes and behavior bring out the traits and actions in others that cause us to become cynical and generalize that "people are no damn good."

Some years ago, when I was new at operating a business in New York City, I had a painful and costly experience in which I was taken to the tune of several hundred dollars I could ill afford to lose. For a long time I brooded over this and nursed my resentment; I decided that all the tales I had heard about business ethics in the Wicked City were true, and that I had fallen among thieves and been royally fleeced.

Then, over a period of time, it dawned on me that the whole episode couldn't have happened if I had displayed even elementary intelligence. My own stupidity had asked for just the treatment I had received and I could not logically blame anybody for my losses except myself.

It is much easier on the ego to believe that we are victims of other people's malice than to admit that we ever behaved like half-wits and thus invited misfortune. One of the hardest phrases to say in this world is: "I've been a fool." Yet there are times when all of us must say these words to ourselves if we are to grow out of emotional babyhood.

Any child can tell you what's wrong with humanity: that people are selfish, stupid, greedy and self-centered. It takes maturity of insight to recognize the basic goodness of people, the tremendous resources and capabilities of human character.

3

WHY SHOULD PEOPLE LIKE YOU?

WHEN I WAS A DREAMY-EYED GIRL of fifteen, I often thought about some day writing the Great American Novel. I could, in my boundless imagination, see the glowing reviews in the book sections of the Sunday newspapers; I could hear the applause; I could smell the incense.

I planned the Paris gowns I would wear; I saw myself being quoted, courted and adored wherever I went. But never, never did I dream of the hard work, the unglamorous drudgery, the blood, sweat and tears that go into any act of creative endeavor. The Cloud Nine I was perched on had room only for the rewards of greatness, not the earning of it.

And so, I never wrote the G.A.N., or any other novel, for that matter. The great books, I soon discovered, were being written by people who were too busy at their literary labors to have any energy left over for dreaming of rewards.

My youthful folly is typical of the state of mind of those lonely souls who walk this earth longing for friends and more satisfying relations with other people. They put the cart before the horse. They want people to like them, but they don't go to much trouble to make themselves likable.

In my own personality-development classes for women, I hear many complaints of "I'm too shy and timid to attract attention;" "Nobody seems to be interested in me;" "People don't care about getting acquainted with me."

Well, why in heaven's name should they? The world is under no compulsion to like you or me or anyone else. Is there any sound reason why people should seek us out, either businesswise or socially, unless we have something they need or desire? What's in it for them?

Confucius once said: "The important question is not are we loved but are we worthy of love."

To attract friendship and affection we must stop worrying about whether people like us or not and concentrate on developing the basic attitudes and qualities that inspire liking and affection.

Marian Anderson has written movingly of an early period in her life when she was overwhelmed with failure and discouragement, when she felt she could never sing again. Gradually, through prayer and soul-searching, she regained her faith and courage to go on with her career. And in a burst of exultation one day, she told her mother:

"I want to sing! I want everybody to love me! I want to be perfect in everything!"

Marian Anderson's mother replied, "That's a wonderful goal. But our dear Lord walked this earth as the most perfect of all beings, yet not everybody loved Him. Grace must always come before greatness."

Miss Anderson was profoundly impressed and she returned to her music dedicated to earning perfection rather than merely longing for it. "Grace comes before greatness."

J. Allen Boone, of Hollywood, California, the keeper of that wonderful dog star of silent movies, Strongheart, learned so much from watching the dog's actions that he wrote a best-selling book, *Letters to Strongheart.* Mr. Boone says the dog had a wonderful, joyful way of executing commands and performing requirements for his motion pictures. The animal did these things, he points out, not for rewards but for love and the pure joy of doing a good job.

There were many times when Strongheart would perform just for fun when nobody asked him to. It was the execution of good work, not the reward for it, which mattered to the dog. And this was the secret of his success as a film star.

Mr. Boone also tells of a young girl dancer who had won an audition and was as nervous as a June bride. She *knew* she would fail! But then he advised her, "Get your mind off the result; do it just for the joy of doing it. Just dance for God."

Her transformation was immediate, and complete.

Yes, the whole secret of winning friends is to quit

worrying about results, whether people will like us or not, and start doing those things which will inspire love and friendship. We might well reflect on the words of Sir William Osler, who wrote: "Our business is not to see what lies dimly ahead, but to do what lies clearly at hand."

One of my husband's closest friends, writer Homer Croy, has a genius for friendship. Every person he meets—street cleaner, millionaire, man, woman or child —feels a warm glow of affection after spending fifteen minutes with Homer. Why? He isn't young, handsome or rich. He doesn't pretend to be sophisticated. But everyone who meets Homer Croy knows immediately that he likes them.

Children climb on his lap. Servants in the homes of his friends work twice as hard to cook a meal for him. And nobody turns down a party invitation if the host says, "Homer Croy will be here!" Apart from the affection of his many friends, Homer Croy enjoys more adoration from his wife, his daughter and his grandchildren than most people will ever know.

His secret of happiness is simple—he sincerely loves people. What they are and what they do have nothing to do with his philosophy. The fact that they are part of the human race is sufficient. When he meets a stranger, Homer immediately starts getting acquainted, not by talking about himself but by asking the stranger all about himself. Where does he come from, what does he do, does he have a family? He's not being nosy; he's genuinely interested in this new acquaintance and he wants to know these things.

I have seen hard-bitten cynics expand like flowers in the sun under this treatment. It is what Ambassador Joseph Grew meant when he said, "The secret of diplomacy can be summed up in five words: 'I want to like you.'"

Homer Croy never worries over making friends. He just *is* a friend to everybody. Whether people like him or not doesn't concern him. He has his mind on liking others, not on the possible results that may accrue to him.

Every experienced salesman knows that worrying about whether or not he will make a sale can cause such a psychological block that he can't make a proper presentation. Harry Bullis, Chairman of the Board of General Mills, years ago worked his way through college by selling sewing machines. Mr. Bullis says the way to be a successful salesman is to forget about the sales you hope to make and concentrate on the service you want to render.

The moment a man's attention is centered on service to others, he becomes more dynamic, more forceful and harder to resist. How can you resist someone who is trying to help you solve a problem?

"I tell our salesmen," says Mr. Bullis, "that if they would start out each morning with the thought, 'I want to help as many people as possible today,' instead of 'I want to make as many sales as possible today,' they would find a more easy and open approach to their buyers and they would make more sales. He who goes out to help his brother man to a happier and easier

193

way of life is exercising the highest type of salesmanship."

In playing golf we are told to keep our eye on the ball. In teaching effective speaking to adults, we tell students to keep their minds on the message they want to get across. Nervousness, fear and poor delivery are by-products of worrying over a result rather than concentrating on the means of bringing about the result.

I have learned this myself the hard way. I am a timid soul, the type who is always intimidated by headwaiters, railway porters and taxi drivers. Public speaking is not my native element. It takes as much effort on my part to stand before an audience as would be needed by the average person to appear before a congressional investigating committee.

On one occasion several years ago, I was treating one of my closest friends to an exhibition of jitters because I had a speech to make before what I considered to be an especially tough audience. "What if they don't agree with me?" I nervously asked my friend. "What if they don't like me?"

"Well," she said, "why should they like you? What are you going to do for them? Do you think your message is important?"

I admitted it seemed important to me.

"Okay," she told me. "I don't see that it matters what they think of you as long as you deliver that message. If you get it across to them, it doesn't matter if they hate you. You've done your job."

That idea changed my whole outlook on making speeches. Whenever I have to speak now, I say a little prayer beforehand: "Please, God, help me to express a thought which will help this audience and give it something to take home." That prayer has helped me and I hope it has also helped my audiences. Certainly it makes me humbly aware of what my real job is as a speaker, not to charm, not to exhibit myself as a person, but to bring, if I can, some stimulation of thought and spirit which will be of value to others.

I believe that we, as a nation, have a complex about being liked and admired that gets in the way of our true functions. We are extremely sensitive about what other nations think of us, not only in affairs of state but as individuals. We spend billions to buy the friendship of other nations and are deeply hurt and amazed when we are still criticized and condemned by the countries who depend on our bounty. As a nation, I often think we are like the poor little rich girl who wants to be loved for herself alone.

All of this bears upon my thesis that friendship, like any other kind of success, must be earned by concentration upon giving, not receiving. It must be won, not merely attracted. The ability to win friends has nothing to do with back-slapping familiarity, life-of-the-party antics, ability to make a fourth at Canasta or tell funny stories well. It is a state of mind, an attitude toward life and people, a desire to give love, interest, attention and service to others.

This sounds suspiciously like what your minister has been saying to you fifty-two Sundays a year. It is. The more modern the world gets, the more practical we find the basic religious truths expounded thousands of years ago.

A. E. Housman, author of *A Shropshire Lad,* was one of Britain's greatest intellectuals—poet, critic, lecturer and teacher. He prided himself on his contempt for church dogma and what he called "religious folklore." Yet, in a lecture at Oxford entitled "The Name and Nature of Poetry," A. E. Housman said this: "I consider these words to be the most profound truth ever uttered by man: 'He who saveth his life shall lose it—and he who loseth his life, for My sake, shall save it.'"

Housman was speaking of art and aesthetics and the necessity for the creative artist to be concerned with creation, not with the possible rewards of that creation. And those words are true of art, of business success, of winning friends, of any phase of human endeavor. We must put first things first. To win love, we must be loving; to win friends, we must express friendliness. To attract the interest of others, we must first be interested in them. There isn't any other way that brings permanent results.

Granted, that in order to win friendship and affection, we must first have the inner attitude of giving rather than receiving. But what then? Well, this attitude to be effective, must be expressed. It isn't enough just to have a heart of gold. The gold must be spent if it is worth anything. "By their fruits ye shall know them."

Take husbands and wives, for example. It is true that a deep, mutual affection doesn't need to be constantly expressed in words. But it is also true that if it isn't expressed in some way it is in danger of drying up for lack of nourishment. And how many times have we heard a wife say that all she wants from her husband is appreciation for the little things she does!

There are many other ways, of course, by which the educated heart expresses the inner attitude that wins friends. There's sensitiveness to the needs of others, generosity, enthusiasm and tact. They all add up to an outer expression of an inner attitude. Friendship must indeed be "won."

Love is the basis of all human development and our relationships with people are a measure of our emotional maturity. We must feel what other persons feel; we must understand that what hurts them hurts us. It's empathy, a feeling *with* people, and it's a basic element in maturity. It is an understanding of the real meaning of brotherhood and the identifying bonds of feeling between people. It distinguishes civilization from savagery, and we must acquire this feeling if we are to bring maturity into our relationship with others.

PART V IN A CAPSULE

MATURITY AND MAKING FRIENDS

Loneliness: The Great American Disease.

People Are Wonderful. Learn to appreciate them.

Why Should People Like You? They will like you if you like

them and develop qualities of warmth that attract others.

HOW OLD ARE YOU?

1

IF YOU'RE AFRAID OF GROWING OLD, READ THIS

"It isn't old age itself I'm afraid of," a friend of mine confessed recently, "it's developing the unpleasant traits that so often come with it: self-pity, whining, uselessness, babyish demands for attention, living in the past and all the rest of the horrors. I'd rather die than be like that!"

Who wouldn't? But here's good news: we don't have to get that way! Barring degenerative mental disorders, there is no reason why you and I shouldn't be as personable, interesting and worth while at eighty—and beyond—as we are at twenty, thirty or forty. Others achieve it. Let's look around the world at some of the outstanding personalities of our time who are living examples of what it means to grow up rather than grow old.

Consider Bertrand Russell, for instance, the peppery

little British philosopher. Now in his nineties, Lord Russell complains that he can't walk more than five miles at a time any more without getting tired! Here is his comment: "Most of the men I have known who have retired from work have died of boredom shortly afterward. A man who has been active, even if he has thought throughout his life that a leisurely existence would be delightful, is apt to find life unbearable without some activity upon which to employ his faculties. I am convinced that survival is easier for those who can enjoy life, and that a man who has sufficient vitality to reach old age cannot be happy unless he is active."

Then there was the late Vittorio Emanuele Orlando, the Italian prime minister who concluded the Peace of Versailles. At the age of ninety-four, Orlando worked ten hours a day as an active member of the Italian Senate, head of a successful law firm, president of the lawyer's guild and professor at the University of Rome.

Dr. Raffaele Bastianelli, one of the world's great surgeons, at ninety, has a daily schedule that would wear out many a younger man. He operates three times weekly in his private hospital, has daily office hours, does research, drives his own car and flew his own plane until World War II. Dr. Bastianelli's vitality is a triumph of the spirit over the flesh, for, since the age of thirty, he has suffered from rheumatic arthritis, a stomach ailment and insomnia.

Benedette Croce, the philosopher, taught, wrote and worked a ten-hour day at eighty-nine, although he suffered a stroke several years previously.

Francesco Nitti, another former prime minister of Italy, also is a ten-hour-work-day man. Nitti is eighty-six.

Lord Horder, physician to the late King George of England, was working twelve hours a day on his eightieth birthday, and taking care of his garden and writing poetry in his spare time.

Older women show the same stamina as the men. Dr. Ellis Helen Boyle, of England, the first woman president of the Royal Society for Medical Psychology, lives in a bungalow without water, gas or electricity. Dr. Boyle, at eighty-four, puts in a full day. She indulges herself in an hour's afternoon nap; but her busy day ends only at 2:00 A.M.

Olivia Rossetti, the famous translator and interpreter, works sixteen hours a day at eighty, then she sleeps soundly for six hours.

In our own country, such energetic oldsters as Arturo Toscanini, that grand old maestro, who retired in 1954 at the age of eighty-seven, from directing the NBC Symphony Orchestra.

There is Carl Sandburg, our midwestern poet, still turning out literary masterpieces at eighty. And Grandma Moses, who took up painting at seventy-eight, became one of our most popular artists and was still busy at her easel at ninety-six.

Not to mention Dr. Anton Julius Carlson, Emeritus Professor of Physiology at the University of Chicago and president of the National Society for Medical Research, now past his eightieth birthday, who is spending nine or ten hours daily studying the problems of aging.

Dr. Carlson's idea of babying himself because of his age consists of cutting his working day down now that he has reached eighty—from fifteen hours to a mere nine or ten.

One could multiply this list of those who are doing great and important work at ages most of us consider advanced.

It is easy to dismiss the evidence of these prominent people by saying that they are exceptions, or freaks—geniuses who bear little resemblance to the rest of us ordinary mortals. But what about others who make no claim to be geniuses or even particularly unusual—except that they refuse to be useless and helpless because of their calendar age?

People like J. W. (Daddy) Johnston, for example, who, at the age of one hundred, works every day as a carpenter in Los Angeles, California. Daddy Johnston thinks nothing of toting hundred-pound rolls of roofing paper up a twenty-foot ladder. He says he doesn't know what it means to be sick.

Or take seventy-year-old Mrs. Leon Wazeter of Trucksville, Pennsylvania. She weighs only ninety-six pounds and has suffered from neuritis and varicose veins for years—she has undergone some thirteen operations in her adult life. But, her son tells me, Mrs. Wazeter has not only maintained a consistently sunny disposition, but continues to do a full day's work every day. She keeps a nine-room bungalow for herself and her husband immaculately clean without outside help, tends an extensive garden of four terraces of beautiful shrubs, trees and flowers, and cooks and bakes delicacies that have made her famous locally.

I remember a man in my own state of Oklahoma, the late W. A. Graham of Pryor, who lived to be over a hundred. Mr. Graham was a multimillionaire and a great benefactor of his community. He remained mentally and physically active at the century mark and enjoyed taking ten-mile jaunts to exemplify his favorite motto: "A man on his feet is worth two on their seats."

William Hall, of New Hampshire, a hundred-odd years old, operates a dairy farm with his son. The son cares for the herd while Mr. Hall Senior cooks all the meals and does the housework.

Mrs. Eunice H. Palmer, of Machiasport, Maine, one hundred and three years old, offers her own recipe to those who would enjoy their later years: "Stay so busy that you don't have time to think about your troubles and ailments."

In spite of having lived longer than most, none of these people show any signs of senility or "second childhood," or any of the unpleasant features we often, in our ignorance, associate with old age. Instead, they exhibit what Dr. Martin Gumpert calls "a second prime of life"—a sort of resurgence of vigor after seventy.

"Old age develops a creative urge and power of its own," writes Dr. Gumpert, "of which we have hardly taken notice up to now. . . . And I wonder whether life as a whole will not be richer and happier for all of us once we start discovering the unknown treasure of old age."

If others can lick the bogey of age—can grow up instead of merely growing old—so can you and I, if we eliminate useless fears and concentrate on the attitudes that promote growth of mind and maturity of spirit. We can keep our minds young and vigorous even if our bodies deteriorate. And it will help us to remember what sociologist David Riesman says: "In the case of someone like Bertrand Russell or Toscanini, an essential aliveness of spirit reflexively keeps the body alive. . . . Freud could continue to live with vigor in the face of cancer of the mouth which made eating embarrassing and difficult; as his life went on, he grew steadily more alive and more independent."

Yes, researchers continue to pile up evidence which forces us to revise our previous notions of old age as a time of decay and helplessness. Instead of a tapering-off process of our powers, it can offer renewal of our creative energies and a flowering of personality undreamed of in our youth. If we accept maturity—"growing up"—as our goal, we may truly realize the promise of later years as expressed by Robert Browning: "The last of life, for which the first was made."

2

HOW TO LIVE TO BE 100
AND LIKE IT

In 1954, two physicians, Dr. Flanders Dunbar and his brother Francis, headed an investigation unique in medical research. It was a study of centenarians, people who have reached the age of 100. It seems there are about 1580 men and women 100 years old or older in the United States. The Dunbars and their associates made an intensive study of twenty per cent of this group.

Their findings, reported at the Third Congress of the International Association of Gerontology in London, upset some preconceived notions about old age.

According to the Dunbar report, heredity has little to do with whether or not you will live to be 100. But your personality and emotional make-up have a great deal to do with it. If you have normally good health and are independent, courageous, friendly, loving and fond of your work, you have a good chance of reaching the century mark—and being able to enjoy it when you get there.

All of the centenarians studied by the Dunbar staff were in reasonably good health, eager about life, able to look after themselves and more interested in living than they were fearful of death. Except in years, these people actually weren't old at all.

To me, the Dunbar report proves one thing conclusively: that there is no such thing as "growing old"— we become old only when we stop growing.

This continuing process of growth determines our maturity. When we stop learning, stop improving as human beings, we are finished, old, washed up and ready for the rocking chair or the scrap heap, no matter what our birth certificate says. We are sliding downhill in a hand basket, as my grandmother used to say. It can happen in our twenties or our sixties; numerical age has nothing to do with it.

The Dunbar report on centenarians showed a definite relation between healthy, happy old age and certain attitudes of mind and spirit.

One feature all of the centenarians had in common was keeping busy. In fact, the Dunbars did not find a single retired-to-do-nothing person who has lived to be 100! They concluded that: "Retirement and enforced education in leisure defeat their own goal. Those who remain healthy after age sixty-five wish to work, and they stay healthy because they work." Although many centenarians had retired from one job, they invariably replaced it with some other kind of work.

Emotionally, these 100-year-olds, far from being irritable, crotchety, pampered or hard to get along with, were even-tempered, good-humored, free from worry and hypertension. Most of them were unconcerned about their health. One centenarian couldn't give the name of her doctor because, she said, she had never needed one. Another said she caught her first cold at the age of 113 because her grandson insisted on babying her about going out in the rain.

Although the centenarians differed among themselves about what they ate and whether or not they smoked or drank, there were no alcoholics, problem drinkers or chain smokers among them. They were moderate in their habits.

Ninety-eight per cent of centenarians studied had been married; divorce was infrequent. They had more children than the average in the United States, which is 1.6; their average was 3.9, with broods of ten and twenty children not uncommon. They regarded children as a joy, not a bother, and never complained about the problems of raising them.

Independence is another characteristic of the centenarian. Most of them refuse to live with their children, and they are more likely to help support their descendents than to be supported by them.

They are too busy living to worry about approaching death. Many of them talked as though they expected to be around for a good many more years.

They are receptive to change and new ideas. They have many friends, a relaxed and tolerant viewpoint and a sense of humor. They spend little time talking about the good old days.

All in all, the Dunbar study of centenarians holds out hope for the rest of us. Whether or not we live to be 100, we can at least cultivate some of the attitudes which have enabled these people to experience an old age that is a blessing, not a curse.

Physiologists tell us that even our bodies do not age at the same rate of speed. According to a study made at the Baltimore, Maryland, City Hospital by Dr. Nathan W. Shock, "aging is not something that just starts Bang! Age apparently sets in as soon as we stop growing."

And Dr. N. J. Berrill, of Canada's McGill University, says: "No man or woman grows old all in one package, and a man of 65 may have a 40-year-old heart, 50-year-old kidneys and an 80-year-old liver. . . . One man . . . who claimed to be 91 . . . had a nerve-conduction time of a man of 30, a kidney function of the average 60-year-old, the perceptual capacity of one of 80, and the general metabolism of the average 90-year-old group. Obviously, he was young for his years."

We do not need to fear that old age will cause us to lose our intelligence—provided we have any to lose! Dr. Shock, as well as other researchers, has found that old people with high intelligence grow more intelligent with age; whereas "the dumb ones just get dumber."

Although the *speed* at which we learn decreases gradually after sixty, the ability of the mind to function remains unimpaired. Our bodies begin to age almost as soon as we begin to walk, but our mental potency rises sharply until the age of forty and continues to rise thereafter, until we reach sixty, though at a decreasing rate.

"Even at 80," says Dr. Berrill, "the mental standard is still as good as it was at 35. It is a different mind from that of a 35-year-old, but no less valuable. . . . What most of us face as we grow older is not a decreasing ability to learn but the fact that we have become set in our ways and do not want to learn new things. The machinery gets rusty from not being used. Yet, in use, the mind may be a very fine one."

There is no scientific reason why old age alone should make us decrepit burdens to ourselves and society. Some of our faculties may suffer impairment, but not necessarily all of them. Disease may attack us, but then it sometimes attacks the young as well. We may have economic and financial difficulties, but life has problems to be faced and overcome at any age.

"The way most of us waste our adult years is indeed a sorry performance," says Dr. A. J. Carlson, one of America's great specialists on gerontology, "composed of illusions, competitions, stereotypes and narrow outlooks. . . . The result is that at the end of these years, which are meant to be the climax of our life-span, we are only empty shells, and ready to be nasty, ignorant and helpless old men and women, suffering from all the neurotic symptoms of a postmature infantilism."

Properly understood, the twilight years of life should be our richest—the harvesttime when we can enjoy the mellow fruits of experience and distilled wisdom; the time for enjoying certain aspects of life that early struggle, ambition, stresses and strains may have submerged; the time, in short, for enjoying the rewards of maturity.

Science, with its many victories over disease, has lengthened the life of man by some twenty years in the last half-century. And it is now trying to give us knowledge which will help us to enjoy and make purposeful these added years. Shakespeare's "slippered pantaloon," whining in a chimney-corner of life, seems like a ghost of the past compared to the increasing number of vital, upstanding senior citizens of today who have discovered that growing up, not growing old, should be our chief concern.

3

DON'T LET THE ROCKING CHAIR GET YOU

DR. MARC H. HOLLENDER AND STANLEY A. FRANkel, writing in *Today's Health,* tell about an eighty-one-year-old woman in Kansas City who returned a rocking chair her daughter gave her with the curt explanation: "I have no time for a rocking chair. I'm too busy."

Here is a woman who has grasped the secret of growing up instead of growing old. She has learned that work is a basic principle of life, health and usefulness.

If your idea of perfect bliss is endless leisure, if you look forward to retirement spent in a rocking chair, you are living in a fool's paradise. For idleness is man's greatest foe, a hell brew producing only misery, premature decay and death.

Even overwork will not harm you if it is not tension-producing, but too much rest will.

Doctors everywhere are exploding the notion that hard work by itself is harmful and that rest is beneficial. Dr. W. Melville Arnott, Professor of Medicine in the University of Birmingham, England, to name one, comes right out and says that, while too much rest can produce damaging changes to the body, "none of the known effects of work can harm healthy tissues." "Work," he adds, "even hard work, which involves no avoidable hazard, does not interfere with sleep and nutrition . . . and which allows of enough recreation to counteract tedium, is harmless. Indeed, it is beneficial."

Work seems to be one of the factors involved in delaying the effects of old age. Dr. O. Vogt, of the Institute for Brain Study at Neustadt-Schwarzwald, Germany, reported at a recent international conference on old age problems that exercise of the brain cells delayed the aging process. Overwork, far from damaging the nerve cells, actually delays changes due to old age. Dr. Vogt reported the results of microscopic studies he had made of the nerve cells of normal adult human brains, noting the changes due to age. In the brains of two women, aged ninety and a hundred years at their deaths, who had been very active throughout their lives, the aging of these nerve cells of the brain were found to be considerably delayed.

"In addition," stated Dr. Vogt, "in our collection of specimens we have observed no case in which overwork was found to have accelerated the aging of the nerve cells."

No, hard work will not kill you. But worry and hypertension will. Today's ulcer-ridden, hopped-up, supercharged business executive who drops dead in his early fifties is not a victim of overwork, contrary to popular opinion and his wife's conviction. The actual day's work turned out by such a man, in terms of energy expenditure, would be insignificant. But the atmosphere of tension and strain that accompany his efforts, the sleepless nights, the fear of competition and failure, the worry engendered by his environment drain off his vital energy in an emotional rat race. To escape, he often resorts to alcohol, sleeping pills, benzedrine or frenzied exercise on the golf course or handball court. No wonder his body and nervous system finally revolt against such punishment and escape either in death or a mental breakdown.

The shocking fact that more than half of all hospital beds in the United States are now occupied by the mentally ill—more than victims of polio, cancer, heart disease and all other illnesses combined—is indicative that something is wrong somewhere. And that something is not hard work.

As a nation, we have the highest standard of living in the world. Technological and scientific advancement has freed us from much of the drudgery our grandparents, and even our parents, accepted as a necessary part of life. Working conditions have improved steadily even for the most unskilled occupations. Working hours have decreased for salaried workers. Machines do much more of the work that used to be done by man or animals. We have more leisure than ever before. No, we can't blame our plight on hard work.

For work is a necessary condition of man's life, not

merely his livelihood. Without activity, his body atrophies and dies; so does his mind. Work, contrary to ancient belief, is not punishment for original sin—it is the reward, the seal of man's dominion on earth, the symbol of his overlordship. What we call civilization is the visible result of man's need to build, to create, to labor with hands and brain—the expression of one of our most vital urges. Even nations perish without it.

The great Roman Empire, created by an energetic race of farmers, traders, thinkers and doers, crumbled into dust of its own weight when it fell into the idle hands of corrupt and decadent nonproducers—trade, agriculture, commerce, learning, all forms of activity declined. And Rome fell to the busy barbarians.

The new civilization that emerged on its ruins to spread over the western world sprouted from the seeds of a small, despised religious sect called Christianity. The Christians were workers—artisans, small businessmen, even slaves—men whose primary urge to work was hitting on all cylinders.

To me, it seems no accident that the founder of Christianity was a carpenter, nor that he chose his first disciples from among workingmen—fishermen and a tax collector. Christianity's greatest evangelist, Saul of Tarsus, was a tentmaker.

To regard our means of livelihood as merely an unpleasant economic necessity to be endured until death or retirement put an end to our activity is to rob ourselves of one of the great satisfactions of being a human animal. The innate wholesomeness of work, its beneficial effect and therapeutic value, its relation to a person's character—all of this makes work a noble element in our lives.

For all work, in the last analysis, is service, whether it consists of cooking a meal, scrubbing a floor, feeding an assembly line or perfecting a dance step. Its ultimate purpose is to make life better, easier and more joyful. It is creative. And we must visualize this creative purpose if we are either to enjoy, appreciate or profit from the particular work we do.

J. Arthur Rank, the famous British motion-picture producer, says: "Men often forget the basic 'why' of their business. A seat factory is not just to make seats and profits—it is to make seats that people like to sit in. The seat maker who forgets that will wake up some day and discover that someone has literally pulled the seat out from under him—and his profits."

Some people argue that modern industrial civilization has put an end to the creativeness of work, and that there can be no pride in work that is merely mechanical, or so highly specialized that a man must repeat the same motions hour after hour without any comprehension of the whole process of which he is a small part. How can a man feel any personal pride of achievement, they say, when he is a drudge on an assembly line?

I can speak from my own experience about this. At one period of my life I was employed as a statistical typist in a large corporation—one of many. My work consisted of typing, on a typewriter with a specially built long carriage, large financial reports, hour after hour, day after day. Accuracy was of first importance;

speed was second. I cannot say I enjoyed this work. It was hard, monotonous, uninspiring.

But I can honestly say that I felt pride in doing it as perfectly as it could be done. It was highly skilled, though mechanical, work. I felt a sense of satisfaction in achieving a high standard on my job, even though it was such a small part of a vast operation in which I could not share. It contributed to my growth and character by giving me an appreciation of accuracy and a sense of the importance of striving for perfection even in small things.

And I found the truth of G. K. Chesterton's witticism: "The best way of ceasing to be a secretary is to be a very good secretary."

Dr. Carl F. H. Henry, Professor of Theology and Christian Philosophy at the Fuller Theological Seminary in Pasadena, California, believes that the economic life of man—his work experience—should not be a thing apart, but integrated into his total personality and religious outlook. He says:

"What contributes to the elevation and good of mankind is worthy, even though it does not appear romantic nor novel . . . The real drudgery of the worker today grows not alone out of machine-bound or assembly-routine work, but out of a distaste for work itself, and a . . . misunderstanding of the daily task as something lacking all mission in relationship either to God or humanity. . . . The loss of joy in work, and the depressing drudgery of monotonous toil, may not be due to the character of the work itself, as much as to the spirit of the worker or to the surroundings of the job."

In other words, our inner attitude toward our jobs determines largely whether we find them depressing drudgery or satisfying to our souls.

There are bored housewives who regard the daily routine of dishwashing as a piece of menial servitude. Yet, I know of a woman who has found it to be an adventure. Her name is Borghild Dahl. She is a writer by profession, author of an autobiography, as well as a long list of other books and magazine articles. Miss Dahl has been blind for much of her life. After a series of operations on her eyes, she regained partial vision. She says that after this, her daily task of washing dishes became a small miracle for which she thanked God. "I could see a patch of blue sky from my little kitchen window," she said, "and I never tired of seeing the rainbow colors in the soapsuds. After years of darkness, so much beauty to be had in performing a household task was a never-ending source of gratitude."

Unfortunately, many of us, having eyes, see not. Our imaginations lack the maturity of Miss Dahl's, and we fail to grasp the higher values offered us by the work we do.

As a healer, nothing can top the benefits of hard work. Mrs. Rita Johnson of Muleshoe, Texas, says that it saved her from a nervous breakdown.

Mr. and Mrs. Johnson and their two children moved to a 360-acre farm in New Mexico, back in 1941. "It turned out to be a snake pit," writes Mrs. Johnson, "in the literal, as well as figurative sense. It was infested with rattlesnakes. They must have congregated there from all over the county.

"Although we had no electricity, gas or water on our place, lack of conveniences was the least of my troubles. What got me down was worrying day and night over what would happen if one of the family got snakebit. I dreamed at night of running with one of my children in my arms to get help in time. When my husband was working on the tractor in the fields, I was in a state of terror if I lost sight of him for even a few moments.

"This constant fear brought me to such a pitch that I believe I would have had a mental breakdown had it not been for one thing—hard work. It was a necessity, living as we did, and it saved me. I shelled corn to plant our 360 acres until I had calluses on my hands. I made all my children's clothes. I canned more food than we could use in five years. I worked until I was too tired to care about anything except falling into bed—and I had no energy to spare in being afraid of snakes.

"We moved away one year later, without a single accident due to snake bite. I've never had to work so hard since, but I will always be thankful for the conditions that made it necessary that particular year—hard work saved my reason."

Those who have learned, as Mrs. Johnson did, the power of hard work to pull us through a crisis, have a never-failing defense against the slings and arrows of outrageous fortune. The mere *habit* of work is sometimes enough to pull us out of a temporary slump or set back or disappointment. Hard work often sustains people through a disaster, a personal tragedy or loss of a loved one.

Edmund Burke said: "Never despair. But if you do,

work on." Edmund Burke was not theorizing about this —he knew. He had lost a beloved son. His studies had filled him with the bitter conviction that civilization was going down the drain. Work was, to him, as it has been to so many others, a note of sanity in a crazy world—so he kept on working, even in his despair.

Yes, work is a law of life. If we are deprived of it for any reason, we suffer. Work therapy is used in institutions—mental hospitals, prisons, sanitariums, in any place where people must be segregated in numbers. The saying that "retired men die young" is sadly true. Retirement from active, busy usefulness to a twilight world of utter idleness or aimless time-killing stifles the vital principle in all of us, lowers our resistance and often brings on premature death. People who are happiest in retirement are those who simply change occupations.

The outmoded notion that people should be retired from their job at the age of sixty-five is a hangover from horse-and-buggy days and a shame to any nation which prides itself on progress. The retirement-age standard of sixty-five was adopted in 1870 by the Railroad Retirement System, and in 1937 by the Social Security System. Since 1900 our life expectancy has been increased by some twenty years, so that a man or woman of sixty-five today cannot be logically considered ready for the rocking chair or the undertaker. Yet, we are still forcing people to retire when, in many cases, they are at the peak of their usefulness.

An authority on retirement problems is Thomas Collins, feature editor of the Chicago *Daily News* and author of the book, *The Golden Years*. His column entitled "The Golden Years" is syndicated in some ninety newspapers. Mr. Collins regards compulsory retirement as "cruelty." This is what he says:

"It is my observation, based on more than seven years of interviewing people just under and just over 65, that compulsory retirement is a cruelty America would not tolerate if it were inflicted on horses or dogs. Horses at least are turned out to pasture where food can be nibbled. Everybody's dog is fed until he dies.

"But the cruelty lies not alone in the threat to subsistence. . . . It lies in the libel committed against the capabilities of 65-year-old men and women. It lies in the lasting damage that sometimes is done to the spirit of these people.

"For a person ever to be told he is too old for anything, when it is a situation that the angels of heaven can't change, is a terrible thing. For a person ever to be dispossessed of his work, his income, and the source of his pride, by the only society he ever knew, is also a terrible thing. It is a cruelty that is inflicted nowhere in the span of life except at age sixty-five."

Why haven't the people most concerned with this cruelty of arbitrary retirement been consulted, the sixty-five-year-old workers themselves? The plain truth is that the great majority of workers do not want to retire at sixty-five! In the state of Indiana alone it was found that ninety per cent wished to continue working; in certain large factories the percentage ran as high as ninety-five per cent.

Considering the attitude of business and industry towards employing older people, it is heartening to note how many of them go out and hustle up jobs for themselves anyway. According to one authority in the field of social welfare, Julietta K. Arthur, "the most remarkable employment fact to emerge from the 1950 census was the report that hundreds of thousands of men and women *past* seventy-five were still working, many of them self-employed."

The Metropolitan Life Insurance Company published a report in 1954 which indicated that three fifths of all men between the ages of sixty-five and sixty-nine were gainfully employed. The proportion of those men working between the ages of seventy and seventy-four is about two fifths. And one out of every five men of seventy-five years and older is still working. A large proportion of these older workers are self-employed.

These figures point up one big fact—that the capacity, ability and willingness to work do not come to an abrupt end on one's sixty-fifth birthday.

The majority of people want to go on working as long as their capacities permit, not retire because some pension-planner says they should. The resistance of a large percentage of workers to this unfair forced retirement has caused some business firms to sit back and take notice. Some of them have increased their retirement-age ruling or made it more flexible. Unhappily, these firms are still in the minority. How long will it be before the God-given right to work will no longer be denied a person because of his calendar age, regardless of his need, ability and desire?

At a recent conference held by the State of New

York to study the problems of the aging, a telegram was read from the distinguished elder statesman, Bernard M. Baruch. Mr. Baruch, in his telegram, called for an end to compulsory retirement, which, he said, was "no boon to those who, despite their years, are both willing and able to continue working." Retirement should be based not on age but on ability, Mr. Baruch continued. "Older people have acquired the priceless asset of experience for which there is no substitute."

Listen to Dr. Henry S. Curtis who, at the age of eighty-three, is a member of the State of Michigan Commission to Study Problems of Aging. Dr. Curtis, one of the nation's authorities on this subject, boldly speaks out about unfair employment discrimination against our elder citizens:

"Compulsory retirement is a serious wrong to industry because it shelves many of the best men, and takes away the incentive of the employees to do good work during their later years. It is a serious wrong to the worker who is able and wishes to keep on. It is a serious wrong to the public, which has ultimately to pay the bills. The right to work is a fundamental human right; automatic discharge at sixty-five is a fundamental human wrong."

Bravo, Dr. Curtis! May the planners and bureaucrats someday take time out from their graphs and charts and listen to the voice of wisdom and common sense crying in the wilderness of Compulsory Retirement Acts. "The rule of discharge at sixty-five," says Dr. Curtis again, "is arbitrary, for there is no law of physiology or psychology that says a man's working capacity ends then. Weakness and incapacity may come at any age, and at different times for different individuals. . . . If we cease to use our hands, they soon lose their cunning. If we cease to use our brains, we go down the scale rapidly toward senility. There will come a time for every worker to give up his work, but this should come at different times for different people."

Work is one of the joys of maturity unimaginable to the very young. Work, whether it be of the hands or the head, is one of nature's mightiest forces in keeping us growing up instead of allowing us to grow old.

For those who would avoid the perils of old age, the best thing is to follow the advice of the eighty-one-year-old woman in the first paragraph of this chapter: Give back the rocking chair and get busy!

PART VI IN A CAPSULE

HOW OLD ARE YOU?

If You're Afraid of Growing Old, Read This. Learn some of the facts about aging.

How to Live to Be 100 and Like It. To live longer, develop attitudes that promote health of mind.

Don't Let the Rocking Chair Get You. Work as long as you can.

MATURITY OF SPIRIT

1

THE COURT OF LAST APPEAL

In June, 1942, the North African town of Tobruk was taken by the Germans. The attack on Tobruk
started about five o'clock in the morning and continued
through the day. On the eastern perimeter of the town
a South African contingent of the defense was sta-
tioned. Hammered unceasingly by German guns, they
were finally driven out of their position by German
tanks, supported by heavy artillery and dive bombers.
The South Africans retreated to a "wadi," or dried-up
watercourse, and followed it down toward the sea. Sur-
rounded on all sides by the enemy, they still nursed a
forlorn hope of escape from the trap. In the words of
one of those soldiers, this was the position:

"We few survivors staggered on, under the merciless
heat of the desert sun, taking turns carrying our
wounded, conscious of our desperate plight and knowing that if the enemy should reach the edge of the
"wadi" just fifty feet above us we would be sitting

ducks. Fear walked beside us—fear of death, imprisonment and of what our next step through that awful place would bring. Suddenly, for no apparent reason, these words drifted through my mind: 'Yea, though I walk through the valley of the shadow of death, I shall fear no evil, for Thou art with me.' I can't explain it, for I had never been what people call a religious man. Yet, these words from the Twenty-third Psalm seemed to sing themselves over and over to me, and I felt the fear, worry and tension melt away from me, and strength and confidence well up inside me.

"It is hard to find words for what happened when my mind became filled with this thought during that hell march. And hard to explain just how and why the same phrase sustained and comforted me when we were captured and I endured the long years of imprisonment that followed. All I know is that they made me realize that I was not alone, that some higher power stood with me in my suffering. The knowledge is still with me."

The soldier who lived through this dramatic experience is now living in Toronto, Canada, at 40 North Heights Road. His name is Syd Bebbington.

Mr. Bebbington is only one of many who have discovered that there is a Court of Last Appeal, when all human resources have failed. It doesn't matter if you call this power God, Allah or merely second wind—the important thing to remember is that it is as real as physics, and only waiting to be used in times of stress and trouble.

Mr. Bebbington said that he was surprised by this

experience because he had never considered himself a particularly "religious" man. I suppose he meant that he had not had any special church affiliation, nor any interest in theology. A psychologist might tell us that shock and suffering had reduced his physical resources and rendered his nervous system peculiarly sensitive and receptive, so that a chance phrase, remembered from boyhood and lodged in his subconscious, was enabled, by these unusual conditions, to float to the surface and take possession of his mind.

Does it matter how you explain such an experience? The great big wonderful point is that it happens. If we are to mature in spirit, we must recognize the fact that our only real security lies in our relationship with this hidden reservoir of power. Not to know about it, not to use it, is like willfully starving ourselves to death in the midst of plenty.

My files are filled with letters and stories of people who have discovered this great spiritual law when faced with tragedy and difficulties of every kind. I call them my "Court of Last Appeal" files. Here is one of them: It comes from a man named Irving H. Tolsch, 48 Aster Avenue, Merrick, New York:

"In June, 1946, began the darkest period of my life. My wife, Agnes, had just undergone a serious operation. When it was over, the operating surgeon informed me that Agnes had an incurable cancer and that she had only a short time to live, maybe one year, maybe two. I was stunned. My world fell to pieces around me.

"In the month that followed, while Agnes recuperated from the operation, I lived in a nightmare. I couldn't eat, I couldn't sleep. I began to lose weight. Although I tried hard to be cheerful in my wife's presence, she noticed the change in me. One day she said, 'Irving, why are you so unhappy? Don't you have any faith in God? If God, in his infinite wisdom, decides to take me, why should we question his motives? Our life here on earth is such an infinitesimal speck of time, compared to all eternity, that we shouldn't waste a minute of it in despondency. We should think of the eternal life to come.'

"Her courage was so great, her faith so sublime, that it kindled a similar faith and courage in me. A great weight seemed to be lifted from my heart. For the first time in my life, I felt the presence and all-embracing love of a God who was aware of my needs. Agnes lived only four more years, but those four years were among the happiest we had ever known.

"Every night, I get down on my knees and thank God for my blessings, and especially for the gift of faith. With His help, I am prepared to face anything that life may bring, in the joyful assurance of an eternity where I know my loved one is waiting."

Can we question such a testimony? Here is a man who lived four years in the Valley of the Shadow, yet, because of his spiritual growing up during the first impact of sorrow, he says those four years were among the happiest he and his wife had ever known. His personal loss has not crushed him or made him bitter and resentful; it has strengthened and fitted him to live out his life with the greatest possible benefit to himself and others.

Undoubtedly there are spiritual laws in the universe which are no less real than the laws of physics. How do we know they exist? Simply because they have been tested and proven in the great laboratory of human experience for centuries. God never fails mankind, although the reverse is frequently true.

In the ways of the spirit we must grow, learn and develop just as we do in the other areas of life. We must mature in understanding of these spiritual laws if we are to benefit from them.

Mrs. Lola Curtis, 342 Thirtieth Avenue, San Francisco, California, was shocked into a realization that worry and faith do not mix. It happened like this:

Mrs. Curtis, many years ago, hit the jackpot of troubles. Within a few months, both her parents died, her marriage collapsed, and she was left with a small child to raise, a business to run and thousands of dollars in debts to repay. It was wartime, and restrictions and priorities seriously hampered her business. She was troubled about proper supervision for her child while she worked. To make ends meet, she was forced to take a difficult and complicated office job, which added to her feeling of stress.

The climax came when Mrs. Curtis found herself one day on Market Street in San Francisco, without the slightest idea of how she got there, who she was or where she lived. She was terrified. "In that awful moment of horror," she writes, "I could remember only one thing before recollection came flooding back to me. I remembered a wonderful Irish priest at St. Monica's

Church. I knew he could help me. I went to him as quickly as possible.

"He listened to my tale of woe with friendly sympathy. Then he asked me if I prayed about my troubles.

"I said, 'Yes, Father, I pray.'

"He asked, 'Do you worry about these things?'

"I answered, 'Oh, yes, Father, I worry all the time.'

"This kind, gentle man of God stiffened, his Irish eyes lost their smile, and his soft brogue hardened, as he said, in a tone I shall never forget, 'That is the worst insult you could ever give to God. Why do you doubt God's ability to answer prayer?'

"His words were like a shock treatment. In a flash, I realized what I had been doing: I had been praying for help, and at the same time making it impossible for help to reach me through the fearful, worried turmoil of my mind. I learned my lesson then and there. From that day forward, my prayers welled up from a heart full of confidence, hope and the sure knowledge that God knew my problems and would help me solve them. Approached in this way, my problems vanished. Every need I had was supplied. Even financially, the ends not only met but lapped over. Life became a great adventure instead of a tragic experience to be endured."

The wise Irish priest at St. Monica's who set Mrs. Curtis on the right track put his finger on the heart of her problem. Her mental state was not receptive; it was so blocked with fears and worries that nothing else could penetrate. Once she cleared her mind of this rubbish it was open to thoughts of courage, intelligence and love, the qualities she needed to solve her problems.

People who have learned to rely on God for support early in life are fortunate. But better late than never. To many, the busyness of their days, a feeling of intellectual superiority or a notion that religion is only superstition block them off from receiving spiritual help. For these people, God is indeed the Court of Last Appeal, to be considered only when every human resource has failed. Earl D. Moore, 3017 Maplewood Road, Richmond, Virginia, was made even more aware of this in his moment of greatest danger. It started during World War II, when Mr. Moore, an American G.I., was standing on the dock at Southampton, England, waiting to board a transport which would take him across the Channel to France.

"The Red Cross," says Mr. Moore, "was handing out coffee to us that day. A little band of Salvation Army workers was also there, handing out doughnuts and pamphlets to each soldier who received a doughnut. I welcomed the doughnuts and coffee, but I was impatient of anything pertaining to religion at that particular time and I remarked to a buddy that they should be giving us joke books and comics to take our minds off the heavy action that lay ahead of us, instead of religious tracts. I glanced at the pamphlet in my hand before sticking it into my pocket, and a phrase in black type caught my eye. It said: 'Behold, I am with you always.'

"Before we reached France, our ship was torpedoed. Hundreds of men below decks were killed instantly.

The rest of us felt terror strike our hearts as the cry rang out: 'Abandon ship!' It was night. As we looked into the inky blackness, we thought of the men lying below. Their troubles were over. Our fate was grimmer. We would undoubtedly die more slowly by exposure, drowning, or, even worse, by being picked up and taken prisoner by the enemy sub which lurked in the blackness of the night.

"I spent several hours in the water before being picked up by an English ship. During those hours I prayed. I don't pretend that my prayers actually saved my life, but I do know that they reduced my panic and warded off hysteria. I was able to maintain a reasonable degree of calmness.

"As I lay in the hospital after my rescue, a nurse came in and said to me, 'There was nothing we could salvage in your clothing except this piece of paper. I thought it might be something of importance, but I can see now that the sea water has made it impossible to read. In fact, I can only make out one sentence.' 'What is it?' I asked. She walked over to the window, held the paper up to the light and slowly read, 'Behold, I am with you always.'

"The promise of those words, and my knowledge of their truth sustains me today. Whenever I begin to worry, or feel tenseness mounting within me, I just lean back and think them over. I don't pray in the sense of asking for anything. I just—well, commune is the best word I can think of. The hypertension drains out of me, and peace and confidence take its place. Then I am in a position to deal with my problems calmly and intelligently."

Here is another striking instance. It comes from Mr. C. F. Beasley, 141 West 64th Street, Hialeah, Florida. He writes:

"In February of 1950, I was dangling at the end of my rope. Everything had gone wrong for me. I was attending the University of Florida under the G.I. Bill. My wife was in the hospital and had been there for ten days. I was trying to keep things going at home and care for our two children. I was worried about my wife, about passing my college work, since I had missed so many classes. I was broke. Everything I had or could borrow had gone for doctors' bills and medicine. I was so upset I couldn't think straight about anything.

"One night, while visiting my wife at the hospital, she gave me a New Testament which her Sunday-school teacher had given her and asked me to take it home. I got home about eleven and dropped into a chair, completely exhausted. Without thinking, I switched on the radio and, at the same time, I opened the little book my wife had given me. Over the radio, which was broadcasting a Negro religious service, drifted the song: "Take Your Burden to the Lord and Leave It There." My eyes focused on a sentence in the Bible in my hand, and the words leaped out at me: 'Take, therefore, no thought for the morrow; for the morrow will take thought for the things of itself.'

"Suddenly, I realized clearly that here were the answers to my problems. I had done everything I could

237

do. I was utterly helpless to do more. It was time to let God take over; He would show me the way out.

"That night, I slept better than I had in a month. And from then on, everything worked out gradually. My wife was soon well and back home. My financial difficulties were straightened out. I even passed my courses in college. I had cast my burdens on the Lord—and the morrow had taken care of itself."

Part of the poise and assurance of maturity comes from knowing where to turn for the right kind of assistance. Only a fool supposes that he is completely self-sufficient in every emergency. If we need physical help, we turn to a doctor; for financial advice, we go to our banker; when drains are faulty, we call on a plumber. In order to keep growing, to reach out after fulfillment, our spirit needs nourishment, as well as constant repair.

And the great Expert is always on the job to help us if we only have the sense to call on Him. The Court of Last Appeal is always in session.

2

THE FOOD OF THE SPIRIT

A CERTAIN DOCTOR in New York City was talking to me about his experiences doing volunteer work in the hospital for incurables on Welfare Island. This is a multimillion-dollar hospital, fitted out with the most modern equipment and staffed with the finest medical talent. A number of New York doctors donate their services to the patients in this hospital. Only "incurables" are admitted. They come from everywhere.

"When I first began to work in this hospital," said the doctor, "I asked myself why I was there. These patients had no hope of ever again leading normal lives. They were useless to themselves and to society. Shouldn't I be using my energies for patients who had a chance to live? Hour after hour, as I performed my duties among these discarded people and looked at their haggard, wasted faces, the question pounded in my brain. Why was all this money and time being spent on such lost causes?

"One day the answer came to me. It was very simple: these patients are human beings. If a dog is sick or dying, other dogs pass him by, give him a wide berth. This is the great difference between man and the other animals. So long as a human being exists, he has a right to be accorded the dignity that belongs to a member of the human race. He is of concern to the rest of us because he is human. When we no longer have any interest in a person because he is 'incurable,' we lose our own humanity and are no better than animals.

"Hitler forgot this, in his policy of exterminating the old, the insane, the incurables, because they were no longer of any use to his state machine. His nation relapsed into barbarism which shocked the civilized world.

"Realizing that my job as a physician is to do what I can for suffering humanity, regardless of what the chances are for recovery of a patient has not only, I believe, made me a better doctor, but a better human being."

Here is an example of a mature spirit, of what some people call a "religious outlook." It has nothing to do with church denomination or creed, or with observing formal ritual. It is a simple recognition of the fact that man is something more than blood and bones and a mixture of chemicals. It is the answer to the question Jesus asked in the Sixth Chapter of Matthew: "Is not the life more than meat, and the body more than raiment?"

Our value to ourselves and others is largely determined, whether we realize it or not, by our recognition and realization of our relationship to some unseen force which is part of us and yet above and beyond us. Once we understand that we are a part of this great force, our relations with our fellow human beings fall into clearer focus. If we accept the fatherhood of God, we must also accept the brotherhood of man.

A concern for others' welfare is the basis of ethics, as well as of religion. But we cannot do much for others until we have first done something for ourselves, until we have a spiritual core, a center for our lives to give motivation and direction to our activities.

In the words of the late Peter Marshall: ". . . here we are. We have money. . . . We are well clothed. . . . We are comfortably housed. . . . We have automobiles —and all the latest gadgets in our homes. But *we are spiritually undernourished.*"

This spiritual undernourishment is at the root of many of our emotional and mental ailments. It under-lies all areas of emotional immaturity, in the same way that malnutrition stunts physical growth.

The idea that men and women are born with a spir-itual urge as strong as their instincts of sex and hunger is the foundation of a new school of psychiatric thought growing in Vienna today. The leader of this new ap-proach to medicine and psychiatry is Dr. Viktor Frankl, teacher of neurology and psychiatry at the University of Vienna and President of the Austrian Society of Medical Psychotherapy.

Dr. Frankl believes that, while most men and women today have conquered their bashfulness about sexual emotions, they are deeply troubled by repression of their inborn religious feelings. Dr. Frankl calls this repression "God-shyness." It is, he believes, "the real pathology of our age."

To achieve emotional health, people must overcome the notion that religion and God are not real needs and that it is unsophisticated to search for a spiritual side to life. In order for our lives to be meaningful, according to Dr. Frankl, they must be firmly anchored to faith and belief in God as a foundation of life.

Dr. Frankl formulated his idea of "logotherapy," as he calls it—the medical recognition and treatment of the soul—in the Nazi concentration camps of World War II. He found that "even in a concentration camp life can be worth living—and I was a prisoner in three such camps, including Auschwitz and Dachau. The inmates there did not keep sane by dwelling on the ideas with which psychoanalysis has flooded the world. Instead, many of them sought a spiritual meaning in their predicament and learned, through suffering, to draw closer to their God."

If science is beginning to recognize the sick personality's need for God, it is of equal significance to the healthy personality, in its search for maturity and fulfillment, to find meaning in its relationship to God as the great, throbbing heart of the universe.

Prayer is the connecting link through which we become conscious of God as a force in our lives. It is communication, a current which flows both ways, operating between ourselves and the creative principle of all life. It is the key which unlocks the doors of the spirit.

Prayer isn't begging for what we want. It is a relaxation of the soul in which we become receptive, a willingness to accept a higher will than our own. It sweeps the mind clean of negative emotions, thus making it possible for our own positive powers of character to operate.

Emotions of fear, worry, anger and hate clog up our thought processes to the extent that our intelligence and judgment are unable to function. Our lines of communication must be kept clear. Prayer is the agent that clears the trash away so that intelligence is free to operate.

James E. Pence, 1200 West 6th Street, El Dorado, Arkansas, writes of his troubles during the depression-filled years of 1932 and 1933. "I had to quit school," he writes, "in order to help support a partially invalid mother and three younger sisters. I was only a kid myself, and grown men were out of work—what could I do? I hitchhiked the highways and rode freight trains from town to town, working at any odd jobs I could pick up to earn a dollar to send home.

"When the Civilian Conservation Corps was formed, I enrolled. I was able to send $36 a month home to my mother and sisters. This should have made me happy, but it didn't.

"Night after night, I lay in my bunk and cried. Often my pillow was so wet with tears that I would get up early and change the pillowcase before the other boys would notice. My depression centered around the education I feared I would never be able to get, and my having to leave school to work.

"Then I remembered what Grandad often told me

when I was a little boy: 'Son, when you have a problem that seems too big for you, ask God to help you.' I began to pray every night. I didn't have the courage to kneel in sight of the other boys, so I always waited until lights were out and I was in bed.

"Gradually, my nightly fits of weeping stopped, and the burden of regret was lifted from me. I felt better physically and even gained a little weight. A few months later, my prayers were answered: a notice appeared on the bulletin board announcing that boys who wished to continue their schooling might report to a newly appointed educational advisor and discuss their needs.

"This experience taught me that prayer is the answer to every human problem."

Those people who discover the power of prayer early in life, like Mr. Pence, have acquired the greatest technique and the most powerful ally available to mankind for growth, maturity and fulfillment.

Some people discount prayer because they believe their prayers are not always answered. They lack the perception of the little girl who prayed for a pony on her birthday. When her birthday rolled around and the pony didn't appear, her little brother taunted her by pointing out that, since she had asked God for a pony and hadn't received a pony, He obviously hadn't answered her prayers. "He did, too," sobbed the little girl. "God said no!"

Some time or other, God says no to all of us. It is hard for a child to understand why loving parents do not always grant every request. The reasons why may be quite clear to an adult mind, but the child's lack of experience cannot understand them. It is part and parcel of the growing-up process to accept discipline when it is needed, even though our limited vision may not always grasp why we need it.

Prayer, to be effective, must be receptive to a higher will than our own, not an attempt to dictate to God or demand what we want on our own terms.

One of the most moving stories in my files concerns a Lutheran minister's struggle to adjust himself to God's will. This man, Morris A. Thompson, of Concrete, Washington, lost his beloved son in 1949. Father and son were exceptionally devoted; they worked, played and shared religious work together. The boy was stricken suddenly with polio, after attending a Sunday-school teachers' meeting with his father. Two days later, he was dead.

Mr. Thompson was so grief-stricken that his health suffered. His blood pressure mounted. He was afflicted by nervousness. The age-old question of suffering mankind tormented him constantly: "Why did this happen?"

"Then I did what I had so often counseled my parishioners to do," said Mr. Thompson. "I turned to God in prayer. I poured out my sorrow, my feeling of loss and separation, my despair and grief. The cloud began to lift from me, as I turned again to my duties and continued my prayers.

"I still miss my son, but I now realize that I am wiser, better and more able to serve others than if I had never suffered this experience. 'God worketh all things for good.' "

Sometimes we learn more when the answer to our prayers is no. Through suffering we become aware of true values, we see life stripped down to basic essentials, we become more sensitive to the needs of others and come closer to the great truths of existence—in other words, we grow. As Mr. Thompson found out, this spiritual growth is often painful, but it builds a vital something into our character which can't be acquired in any easy way. So, even when God says no, our prayers are still answered.

It is a mistake to attempt to dictate the precise manner in which we want our prayers answered. So often, we are helped in an entirely different way than we had hoped.

While thousands of stories attest to the effectiveness of prayer in helping us when we need help, it is a mistake to regard prayer as something to be used only when there is nothing else to be done, a desperation-inspired cry.

To get the most out of it, we must use it daily. Just as we take deep breaths of fresh air and do a few push-ups on arising, we can wake up and vitalize our mental and spiritual muscles by daily prayer. I know people who get up early enough to read a chapter of The *Psalms* every morning before breakfast. The least we can do is say a daily thank-you for the gift of life itself, and for the blessing of twenty-four hours in which to express ourselves, to work, to love, to learn and marvel.

And, at night, what better way to end the day than to give thanks for the daily bread we have received and resolve to make even better use of the day to come?

Here is an example of how beneficial a daily regimen of prayer can be. It comes from Jacob L. Kooser, a real estate and insurance broker of Connellsville, Pennsylvania.

Mr. Kooser says he is sixty-nine years old, and still working actively at his business. His friends ask him when he is going to quit. Mr. Kooser has no intention of quitting. This is his secret of making his later years fruitful and joyful.

"Every night," says Mr. Kooser, "I breathe deeply when I retire and get a lungful of good fresh air. Then I fill my mind with fresh thoughts, thoughts of peace and courage, health and hope. I tie my thinking to a verse of scripture, such as 'Come unto me, all ye that labor and are heavy-laden, and I will give you rest.' Then I sleep like a baby all night.

"In the morning, when I awaken at my accustomed hour of seven, I do not leap out of bed, but I continue to lie there peacefully for a few minutes, replenishing my mind and spirit with good thoughts. Usually, these thoughts come from the Bible, like 'I can do all things through Christ, who strengthens me.' With this inspiration and motivation, any vague fears I have of old age leave me, and I go about my day's duties with joy. By following this routine, I look forward to spending my remaining years in usefulness and contentment."

Mr. Kooser has found a better old-age insurance than the fabled fountain of youth. He takes a daily drink of the water of life itself. Morning grouches and insomniacs would do well to try Mr. Kooser's recipe.

Speaking before the British Medical Association, Dr. Thomas Hyslop of the Great West Riding Asylum said that the best sleep-producing agent which his practice had revealed to him was prayer.

People who neglect their physical health until a breakdown forces them to go to the doctor learn the hard way that the best cure is prevention. Prayer is the spiritual counterpart of the regular medical check-up. It keeps open our line of supply and communication to Headquarters, it frees us of unnecessary tensions, clears our minds of debris and eliminates the negative thoughts which hamper our progress. Why wait until crisis or disaster overwhelms us to avail ourselves of divine help and guidance? Perhaps some of these troubles might be avoided if we straightened out our minds and emotions daily. Last-ditch prayers of desperation, like deathbed repentance, are better than none, but it doesn't make sense to sacrifice the advantages of building such an important element as prayer into our daily lives.

I, for one, cannot imagine how I would function without it. While some people may regard it as a confession of my own inadequacy, I freely admit that I could never face an audience without praying beforehand that I will be able to give them what they hope to receive. It helps me to calm my nerves, sharpen my wits and concentrate on my message. Whether I am facing a business conference, writing an article or just doing a routine day's work, prayer conditions me for whatever effort is necessary. If I feel under pressure and full of tension, I remember the words from the Psalmist: "Be still, and know that I am God." It works better than a steam bath and massage. On a fine day, the words: "The heavens declare the glory of God, and the firmament sheweth His handiwork" well up out of memory to touch the heart with magic. Prayer points up the real values in living, so that we see the world through eyes aglow with enthusiasm, wonder and delight. It keeps the dust from settling on the spirit.

Most of all, prayer fills us with awareness of the constant presence of God, in all our activities, waking or sleeping, at home or abroad. We are never alone. In sorrow, we are comforted; in danger, we have courage; in despair, we have hope. "If I take the wings of the morning, and dwell in the uttermost parts of the sea . . . even there shall thy hand lead me. . . ."

There can be no true maturity without wisdom of the spirit. A child's mind in a man's body can be dangerous. The history of civilization is the history of mankind's awakening, slowly growing conscience. Man has matured first in other ways. Technologically, materially, scientifically, he has reached undreamed-of accomplishments. Spiritually, he is still a child. He does not know how to govern himself or his fellows, nor how to live in the same world with them peacefully. He has knowledge, but not wisdom. The dilemma of our century is that we are faced with the necessity of growing up or blowing up.

Only by growing up as individuals, by desiring wisdom of the soul, by putting away childish things and accepting the responsibilities of adulthood can we in any way affect the shape of things to come. A nation composed of mature men and women might conceivably rise to the great necessities of our time. What you and I think and what we do—our habits of mind, spirit, thought and action—are important in a larger sense than we realize. What we are as individual human beings has some kind of effect upon every other person with whom we have contact. And what we are can be fashioned by prayer.

PART VII IN A CAPSULE

MATURITY OF SPIRIT

The Court of Last Appeal. When all else fails, try God.

The Food of the Spirit. Our spirit is nourished through prayer.